Part of the "Inside Tuscany: A Second Time Around" series.

Central Tuscany: Best of Cortona

Enjoy the Hill Town of Cortona

2020 / 2021 Edition

Scott Tiezzi Grabinger

2020

Verso

First published in 2012.
Third Edition: May 2016.
Fourth Edition: January 2018
Fifth Edition: February 2019
Sixth Edition: November 2019
Copyright © 2020 R Scott Grabinger, LLC. All rights reserved.

No part of this publication may be reproduced, stored in a retrieval system, or transmitted in any form or by any means electronic, mechanical, photocopying, recording or otherwise without the prior written permission of the author.

Seek permissions from Scott Grabinger.
Email: Scott.Grabinger@gmail.com

Please help me keep this up-to-date, send any corrections and recent news to: Scott.Grabinger@gmail.com.

Color Digital Edition Available. If you would like a color pdf copy of this book please send me an email with the copy of your receipt and I'll email the color pdf back to you.

ISBN-13: 978-1523860821
ISBN-10: 1523860820

v. 6.1

Registered trademarks

® Inside Tuscany Tours
® Inside Tuscany
® "A Second Time Around" series

Cover Photos:

- An antipasto of *burrata* cheese, fresh tomatoes, and arugula at the Trattoria la Grotta.
- An Etruscan altar at the excavation of Sodo II at the base of the Cortona hill.
- A fountain near Chiesa di San Domenico in Cortona.

Inside Tuscany Books by Scott Tiezzi Grabinger

In-Print Tuscany Guidebooks on Amazon

Central Tuscany: Arezzo
Central Tuscany: Eight Tuscan Hill Towns
Central Tuscany: Le Crete and the Val d'Orcia
Central Tuscany: The Casentino and Valtiberina
Central Tuscany: Best of Cortona

Traveling in Tuscany Memoir: Essays and Stories

Walking The Aqueduct: Tuscan Adventures and Culture

Find these books for your iPad or phone on Apple's Books

Inside Tuscany: Arezzo Churches
Inside Tuscany: Arezzo Museums and Sites
Inside Tuscany: Best of Cortona
Inside Tuscany: Driving in Italy

Social Media Sites

Email Contact: scott.grabinger@gmail.com
Facebook: www.facebook.com/scott.grabinger
LinkedIn: www.linkedin.com/in/scott-grabinger-3890b073

Book Descriptions: www.stgbooks.com
Photo Galleries: www.stgimages.com

SECTIONS

Inside Tuscany Books by Scott Tiezzi Grabinger	iii
Dedication	viii
I Tuscany	9
II Cortona Sites	21
III Eating, Sleeping, and Events in Cortona	109
IV Information	123

RECIPES

Osso Bucco	10
Acquacotta	27
Broccoli e Fagiolini (Broccoli and Green Beans)	32
Chocolate Mousse	76
Veal Cutlets Braised in a Simple Tomato Sauce	88
Marisa's Lemon Cake — Torta Limone	96
Pasta with Fresh Tomatoes	114

MAPS

Map of Cortona	24
The Plan of the Fortezza di Girifalco	106

Table of Contents

Inside Tuscany Books by Scott Tiezzi Grabinger	*iii*
Sections	iv
Recipes	iv
Table of Contents	*v*
Dedication	*viii*
I Tuscany	*9*
1 Basics	*11*
Returning to Tuscany	11
Basic Assumption: You've Passed European Travel 101	11
Websites: English and Italian	11
GPS	11
Costs, Getting Money, and Debit Cards	12
Credit Card Strategies	12
Italian Oddities	13
Photography Practices	14
Photo Credits for This Book	14
How to Follow My Descriptions of Churches	14
Comportment in Churches	15
Recipe and Food Information	15
2 Inside Tuscany's Principles for Slow Travel	*17*
Principle 1: Go slow and easy. Plan to return	17
Principle 2: Adapt and learn new things	17
Principle 3: Travel cheap	17
Principle 4: Come to "tour" and to "live."	17
Principle 5: Put your camera down and look around	18
Principle 6: Fly under the radar.	18
Principle 7: Does €25.00 really matter?	18
Principle 8: Pack light, walk easy.	18
3 Set Up a Base and "Live" for a Few Days	*19*
"Live" for a couple of days	19
What should I consider in South Central Tuscany?	19
It's All About the Caffè	20
II Cortona Sites	*21*
4 Cortona Background	*23*
Legends of the Beginnings of Cortona	25
5 Piazza Repubblica and Palazzo Comunale	*29*
6 Piazza Signorelli	*31*
7 MAEC	*33*
Highlights	34

MAEC Rooms A-E	40
8 Melone il Sodo Excavation	51
9 Museo Diocesano — Diocesan Museum	53
10 Duomo della Santa Maria Assunta	69
Interior	70
11 Chiesa di San Domenico	77
Interior	77
12 Chiesa di San Francesco	83
Interior	84
13 Santuario di Santa Margherita	89
Walking to the Basilica — Two Trails	90
Interior	92
14 Chiesa di San Niccolò	97
15 Chiesa di San Cristoforo	99
16 Other Churches in Cortona	103
Chiesa di San Marco	103
Chiesa di Sant'Antonio Abate	103
Chiesa della Santa Maria Nuova	104
L'Ermeo di Celle	104
17 Fortezza di Girifalco	107
III Eating, Sleeping, and Events in Cortona	**109**
18 Sleeping in Cortona	111
Locanda Pretella Hotel 26	111
Rugapiana Vacanze	112
19 Eating in Cortona	115
Trattoria La Grotta	115
Caffé degli Artisti	117
Ristorante La Loggetta	118
Ristorante Il Cacciatore	119
20 Cortona Events	121
IV Information	**123**
21 Travel Information	125
Water, Wine, and Picnics	125
Transportation	125
Using the Phone	126
Electricity and Battery Charging	127
Internet Access — Hotspots	128

Check with your own cell phone company before you go to see if you can use your cell as a hotspot. I use T-Mobile and often use it to connect because when wifi is unavailable. The speed, though is usually 3G speed. It is rare to get 4G speeds. 5G?

Hopefully in my lifetime. Painful. 128
Medical Help 128
Strikes (Sciopero) 128
Overnight Options 129
Banks, Foreign Exchange Bureaus and ATMs 129
Before You Leave Home: Packing 130
Documents for Traveling in Italy 130
Automobiles 130
Opening Hours: Sites, Shops, and Restaurants 131
Post Office 132
Polite Cultural Practices when Shopping 132
Kinds of Restaurants 133
Basic Courtesies 134

22 *Wine Tasting in Italy* 137
Tasting Protocols 137
Tasting 138

23 *Decoding Religious Art* 143
Themes 143
Saints and Their Symbols 149
Church Classifications 154
Relics of Saints 156

24 *Author: Scott Tiezzi Grabinger* 157

25 *Index* 161

Dedication

For Addie, Luke, Bailey, and Grace.

1 Tuscany

Riders in the Giro d'Italia.

> *Like all great travellers, I have seen more than I remember, and remember more than I have seen.*
> Benjamin Disraeli

Osso Bucco

The key to this dish's rich sauce and flavor is the *odori*.

Ingredients

4 large veal shanks cut 1 to 1-1/2 inch thick
2 sprigs of fresh rosemary
2 T lemon zest
3 c chicken or vegetable broth
1 c flour for dredging the veal shanks, salt and pepper to taste
EVOO
twine

Odori and Sauce

3 stalks minced celery
3 minced carrots
1 minced medium onion
1 large can crushed tomatoes
1 handful minced parsley
EVOO
1 c dry white wine

Directions

- Wrap the twine around the veal shanks to hold them together while cooking.
- Heat a heavy, oven proof frying pan (a Dutch oven is great) to medium high, add 1/8 c EVOO.
- Pat the shanks dry with a paper towel and then dredge the shanks in the flour. Place the shanks in the pot (don't crowd) and brown on both sides. Remove the shanks and set aside.
- Add more oil to the pan and sauté the celery, carrots, onion, and parsley over medium to low heat for at least 20 minutes.
- Add the white wine and cook until evaporated while deglazing the pot.
- Add the tomatoes, rosemary sprigs, and lemon zest and stir well.
- Place the shanks on top of the mixture and add enough broth to go half way up the sides of the shanks.
- Cover and roast for three to four hours at 300°. Check frequently to make sure that liquid is half way up the sides of the shanks, add a little more broth or water, if necessary.
- Carefully remove the shanks to a serving platter with a spatula so they don't fall apart and cut off the twine. Spoon some of the sauce on top of the shanks.
- Put the rest of the sauce in a bowl and serve it with the shanks.

I think that orzo pasta is an excellent accompaniment because it absorbs the juices from the sauce and the veal that are on the plate.

1 Basics

RETURNING TO TUSCANY

You've seen Tuscany's top attractions and now you've returned to take a slower pace and absorb more of the culture. This guide takes you to Cortona, one of Tuscany's most beautiful small hill towns. This guide helps you ...

Ruins of an old farm house on a hill above a wheat field near Cortona.

- set a **reasonable pace** to get the most out of your visit,
- **decide** if a site is something that you want to see,
- try a few authentic family **recipes**,
- learn whether a site is **accessible**, and
- find your way with **GPS coordinates**.

BASIC ASSUMPTION: YOU'VE PASSED EUROPEAN TRAVEL 101

Rather than write a "travel book for dummies," I assume that you have passed European Travel 101 and can use buses and trains, read maps, get cash from an ATM, and find basic information at the TI and on the internet. Once you have traveled, you know how to find good local hotels and restaurants on your own and though I include a few, I don't have to use valuable space writing about the same thing dozens of other guidebooks cover and that need revising every few months.

WEBSITES: ENGLISH AND ITALIAN

Most of the websites included in the chapters are in Italian. You can translate the sites with Google Translate and find pertinent information.

GPS

My GPS coordinates are in decimal WGS 84 format from the app *Solocator* on my iPhone. A GPS sometimes gets confused in the small Italian hill towns with their short, curvy, narrow streets. If Apple Maps doesn't work try the Google Maps app. Between the

Ponte Buriano, not far from Arezzo is the bridge that da Vinci painted in the background of the Mona Lisa.

two of them I have a 90% success rate.

Costs, Getting Money, and Debit Cards

Exchange Rates

Prices are in euros; you'll need to find the current exchange rate. As of fall 2019 it was about $1.15 (including bank fees) for €1.00. Thus €20.00 = $23.00. It's best not to think about it.

Getting Cash, Debit Cards, and ATMs

I never buy euros in the US, the fees and exchange rate are outrageous. So, I use ATMs with my debit cards. In fact, you can go to Italy without euros and pick some up at an ATM at the airport. Different banks charge different fees, including your own.

Credit Card Strategies

The Smart Chip

Make sure that your credit cards have smart chips. Europe adopted the technology several years before the USA and you may not be able to use your credit card without a chip. Additionally, Europe updates its technology more frequently, so you can never be 100% sure that a card issued in the USA will work so carry back-up cash and cards.

Fees Mount Up

I use a credit card from Chase Bank that does not charge me a fee for international purchases. Look for a bank card with that benefit. Make sure you know the PIN for your card because some establishments require it.

CALL YOUR CREDIT CARD PROVIDERS BEFORE LEAVING!

Let your card company know that you are going to Italy or they may freeze the card because they suspect fraud; then you'll have the hassle of calling them and letting them know where you are at the moment of purchase.

ITALIAN ODDITIES

TIME: 24-HOUR CLOCK

I use the 24 hour clock in the book. For example, 6:00 am is 06.00 and 11:00 am is 11.00. After the noon hour simply add twelve to the conventional clock: 1:30 pm is 13.30 and 7:00 pm is 19.00.

FLOOR COUNTING

In Europe, the USA 1st flour is the "G" Ground floor. Our 2nd floor is Europe's 1st floor.

OPENING AND CLOSING HOURS AND OFF DAYS

Almost all sites in the smaller, less visited towns close for the lunch hours that begin anywhere between 12.30 and 13.30. The most common closing time is between 13.00 and 15.00. Plan your daily itinerary around the dead time; bring a picnic or go to a restaurant for *pranzo* — Italian for "long lunch."

Every site, except churches, closes one day a week. Usually it is Monday or Tuesday, the same day for all sites in a town.

QR code on a sign at the Girifalco Fortezza in Cortona.

QR-CODES

More and more sites are providing QR-codes to provide you with more information. However, often those museums are buildings with 2-foot thick stone walls that interfere with reception. I see a lot of QR codes, I try a lot of them and don't find many that work.

FREE MUSEUM DAYS

Effective 1 July 2014, State museums announced:

- All State museums are free the first Sunday of the month. It will mean a very busy day at the museum so order tickets in advance.

- Everyone under 18, no matter nationality, is free at any time.

PHOTOGRAPHY PRACTICES

I let you know if a site permits photography. Most sites deny permission. First, because churches and museums claim that the flash can damage paints and most people don't know how to turn off the flash. Second, museums can make money selling books and postcards.

However, national museums have made a change . . .

PHOTOGRAPHS AT NATIONAL MUSEUMS

Finally after years of prohibiting photos the museums are loosening up. In the Italian National museums:

- Photos are allowed as long as you use no flash, tripods, monopods, or "selfie" sticks.

A list of Tuscan state museums can be found at:

>   https://www.discovertuscany.com/tuscany-museums/state-museums-in-tuscany.html

Since the state museums have adopted this practice more and more local museums are also permitting photos under the same rules.

PHOTO CREDITS FOR THIS BOOK

NOTE: Benefit for book purchasers: free color pdf copy of the book.

Except where noted, I took the photos in the book. When a museum forbade photos I found many from the Web Gallery of Art (WGA) (http://www.wga.hu/index1.html) or Wikimedia Commons (WMC) (https://commons.wikimedia.org/wiki/Main_Page), pictures in the public domain. Sorry they are black-and-white in the book, but with on demand publishing, a color book would cost over $35.00.

NOTE: If you have purchased this book, send me an email (Scott.Grabinger@gmail.com) and I will send you a color pdf copy.

HOW TO FOLLOW MY DESCRIPTIONS OF CHURCHES

When I write about a church, I begin at the right wall nearest the entrance, move down the wall to the front altars, across the altars, and then return to the entrance walking along the left wall.

COMPORTMENT IN CHURCHES

- Dress appropriately: wear pants or shorts that extend below the knees and shirts that cover bare shoulders — men and women.
- Turn off phones.
- Only take pictures when permitted and never during services.
- Turn off your flash if flash photography is not permitted. Raise your ISO.
- Do not visit during liturgical services unless participating.

Fresh EVOO that just came out of the crusher an hour before serving with bread toasted over a wood fire and young pecorino cheese at my cousin's Giovanni and Antonella.

RECIPE AND FOOD INFORMATION

I've included recipes, many from my Italian family. They specify amounts and measures of ingredients, but to be honest, they are estimates. My family never measures precisely. As France Mayes put it:

> *"There is no technique, there is just the way to do it. Now, are we going to measure or are we going to cook?"*
> *(Under the Tuscan Sun)*

EVOO MEANS "EXTRA VIRGIN OLIVE OIL"

EVOO has a strong flavor of olives. The best is cloudy which means it came straight from the crusher. Most EVOO in the US is bland and probably counterfeit. You don't want to use EVOO for every day frying and sautéing. Use it on toasted bread for *crostini*, salads, and pasta when you want that pure taste of olive oil.

PECORINO TOSCANO CHEESE — NOT PECORINO ROMANO

When recipes call for pecorino cheese they often say "pecorino romano." It is a common cheese made in America as well as Italy. Easy to find and not too expensive it smells like dirty shoes and tastes worse. Use "pecorino toscano."

Pecorino toscano (from the Italian *pecora*, for sheep) is one of the most prized food products from Tuscany, especially from the Val d'Orcia region. It's harder to find in the US and it is expensive. If you grate it for recipes it goes a long way, though it is delectable as an eating cheese, especially with fruits and marmalades.

If you can't find *pecorino toscano* use parmigiano reggiano — from Italy, not Wisconsin. I have also used young Manchego cheese (sheep cheese from Spain) with excellent results.

Pasta Water

American recipes usually call for gallons of boiling water to prevent the pasta from sticking. A myth. My cousin usually cooks eight ounces of pasta in a quart of water. For a pound of pasta fill a pot with two to three quarts. Throw in a handful of salt to bring out the pasta's flavor. If you stir frequently your pasta will not stick.

Cook the pasta to *al dente*. Everyone says this. What does it mean? Firm but not crunchy.

The salted pasta water also pics up flavor from the dissolving pasta while cooking. If your pasta sauce seems too thick add a few tablespoons of pasta water to make it thinner.

Pasta to the Sauce

I don't think that I've ever seen my relatives add sauce to the pasta. Instead the sauce is in a large pan over low heat to which they add the pasta. This ensures that the pasta does not get cold in a colander. It also helps cook the sauce into the pasta.

The pool at the agriturismo Il Palazzo a short distance in the pleasant country side from Arezzo.

2 Inside Tuscany's Principles for Slow Travel

PRINCIPLE 1: GO SLOW AND EASY. PLAN TO RETURN.

Slow travel is where it's at. Focus on a few things in depth rather than many things lightly. Rushing from one place to another for 10 to 20 minutes gets in the way of true appreciation of the culture. You have to believe that you will return and that quantity of sites doesn't equal quality of trip.

PRINCIPLE 2: ADAPT AND LEARN NEW THINGS.

Trying new things leads to adventures and stories that you'll never forget. Remember that it is not our hosts' responsibility to make things "just like home" — give up the catsup — it's our responsibility to enjoy the differences and to make their home ours.

PRINCIPLE 3: TRAVEL CHEAP.

Expensive franchise, four-star hotels, and tourist-based restaurants shelter you from the local people, culture, and best food. They prey upon your insecurities. (The number of stars in a hotel's name relates to how many services the hotel provides, not cleanliness.) Take a leap: use the one, two, or three star hotels and look for the less expensive restaurants where locals eat. So what if the menu is not in English — go for it. The fewer euros you spend, the more you need to interact with people and the more fun you have. It costs nothing to join the evening passeggiata, but it is an unforgettable experience.

PRINCIPLE 4: COME TO "TOUR" AND TO "LIVE."

When touring, do everything you can to be a "local," to live there. Put your clothes in the drawers, closets, and wardrobes — even just for a couple of nights. Walk slowly through the streets looking for restaurants. Shop for meats, cheeses, and wines for a picnic. Look around and tell yourself, "I live here." Use a base to reduce wasted time moving from place-to-place and to get to know a place well.

Principle 5: Put your camera down and look around.

Pictures are nice — memories are better. It's a richer experience to see through your naked eyes first rather than in a viewfinder. Skip the selfies, which irritate the hell out of everyone around you and for heaven's sake do not use a selfie stick! Don't wait to see your vacation until you watch the video at home or on YouTube.

Principle 6: Fly under the radar.

We Americans often shock our hosts because in our excitement we tend to be loud in voice and dress. Never hide the fact that you are an American but fly under the radar. Leave your baseball caps at home. Locals don't wear T-shirts with advertising. Be humble and respectful in actions, low in voice, and dress appropriately to earn our hosts' respect and gratitude. Ask about the culture. Trust your waiter and ask, "What is best today? What do you recommend?" Enthusiasm for the culture and asking for advice wins people over.

Principle 7: Does €25.00 really matter?

Money flows like water while traveling and it's possible to get too obsessed by it. You may decide to forgo a restaurant meal for a couple of pizzas and drinks for €25.00. A three-course meal for two at an authentic local restaurant might cost you €50.00. One month later, when you are home, will you really worry about that €25.00? Or, will you wish that you'd tried that restaurant?

Principle 8: Pack light, walk easy.

No one ever returns home from a trip and says, "I wish I'd packed more." I live out of a carry-on for two months. You want to be flexible and to travel quickly without dragging 100 pounds of large suitcases to the hotel. Lay everything out on the bed before you leave and put half of it away — then do it again. You'll probably never see those people again and they don't care whether you've worn the same shirt and pants five days in a row and washed out your underwear in the evening.

Take light clothes of synthetic fabrics (make sure that they are breathable) that you can wash easily in the sink and that will dry fast — I've learned to leave my cotton knit shirts and jeans home. I have found that a shirt that is only 50% cotton dries quickly and is very comfortable.

3 Set Up a Base and "Live" for a Few Days

"LIVE" FOR A COUPLE OF DAYS

The best way to see the richness of Tuscany is to set up a base so you don't lose time every day moving in and out of hotels.

A base often has unknown advantages like...

Making fried polenta at the Rigutino Polenta festival in October between Cortona and Arezzo. A great reason to set up a base when visiting Tuscany.

- watching a local weekend festival in medieval costume.
- shopping at a monthly antique fair.
- walking or driving slowly through the rolling hills of Le Crete and taking stunning pictures in the morning or evening light.
- picking up picnic supplies at the weekly market.
- finding a *sagra*, a food festival on the weekend, such as the polenta sagra in Rigutino the first two weekends of October.
- walking with the residents in the evening *passeggiata* before dinner.
- taking a break at a local gelateria.
- finishing the day off with an authentic Tuscan meal at an *osteria* visited mainly by locals.

WHAT SHOULD I CONSIDER IN SOUTH CENTRAL TUSCANY?

Look for medium sized towns. Use Arezzo or Cortona for the Valdichiana. Pienza, Montalcino, or Montepulciano are great for the Val d'Orcia. Look on the web for B&Bs, *agriturismi*, and hotels.

A large place like Siena can be a great place to stay but for me it is too big: swamped by tourists during the day, and fraught with parking problems — a bit of a zoo.

It's All About the Caffè

II Cortona Sites

Scott and Jill at the l'Eremeo di Celle outside the Cortona walls.

The whole object of travel is not to set foot on foreign land; it is at last to set foot on one's own country as a foreign land.
G. K. Chesterton

Parking in Cortona

To put it mildly — it's a bitch!

There are small lots scattered around the walls of the town. If you arrive before 9:00 you'll find something. After that it is a game of musical chairs, being in the right place at the right time when someone else pulls out.

Don't even think about parking inside the walls. There are only a couple of places open to the public, probably all filled by 7:30 am.

I have a secret backup, La Chiesa della Santa Maria Nuova (43.278799, 11.989157) has a large parking lot. Though outside the walls, it is just a short walk up a steep hill to the nearest gate through the walls.

If you don't mind the exercise the Basilica di Santa Margherita at the top of the Cortona hill has lots of space. It's an easy walk down the hill to the tourist area. It's a steep hike back up the hill.

Check:

- http://www.en.cortonaguide.com/cortona_22.html
- http://www.cortonaweb.net/en/maps/cortona-map

4 Cortona Background

Cortona sits on the southern side of Monte Sant'Egidio (3467 ft). The city drops from 2135 ft at the Fortezza to 1515 ft at Porta Guelfa. It was one of the major Etruscan cities from the eighth through fourth centuries BC. In legends it is called the "mother of Troy" and "grandmother of Rome."

Location:

43.274081, 11.987754

Tourist Information:

Via Nazionale 42
0575.630352

The campanile of San Cristoforo near the top of the Cortona hill.

The web sites below provide information on visiting Cortona, including maps of Cortona that show nearby hiking trails, city maps, and parking locations for download:

City Home Page: http://www.cortonaweb.net/en/home

City Center and Parking: http://www.en.cortonaguide.com/cortona_22.html

Third Party Website: http://www.travelingintuscany.com/english/cortona.htm

Time for a visit: To do Cortona justice, take at least a whole day including a stop for a nice *pranzo* at *Trattoria La Grotta* (see chapter 19). It could easily fill two relaxing days.

Reasons for a visit: *Museo Diocesano, Museo dell'Accademia Etrusca e della Città di Cortona* (MAEC), views from the hill, and several fine churches. Home of Renaissance master painter Luca Signorelli.

Accessibility: Difficult. The streets are steep and rough. The main museum, MAEC, has excellent access within its four floors of displays. Some churches have several steps to climb before the entrance.

Map of Cortona

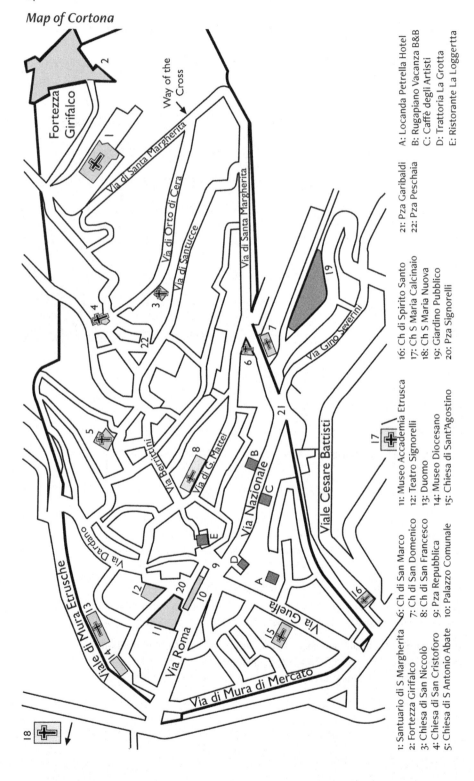

[**Note:** I limited myself to churches and sites that seem to have regular hours and that you can depend on being open. Most small churches are permanently closed or have limited, irregular hours.]

HIGHLIGHTS

Cortona has always been an important hill town; interest seems to have multiplied ten times since publication of Frances Mayes' book, *Under the Tuscan Sun* (1997) — If you are looking for some advance reading, I highly recommend it. Cortona has two of the best museums in Tuscany and art treasures in churches.

Four religious buildings of note are the eleventh century Duomo of Santissima Maria Assunta, the thirteenth century Gothic churches of San Francesco and San Domenico, and the Basilica of Santa Margherita, patron saint of Cortona.

To boil it down further, there are two "absolute must sees." First, the Museo Diocesano, across from the Duomo, has a small collection of outstanding works from the twelfth through twentieth centuries, especially works by Luca Signorelli. Second, visit the Museo dell'Accademia Etrusca (MAEC) that houses artifacts from the fifth century BC to the seventeenth century with a special room for native son modern twentieth century artist, Gino Severini.

LEGENDS OF THE BEGINNINGS OF CORTONA

THE BIBLE

One legend traces the history of Cortona back thousands of years. The seventeenth century *Guida* by Giacomo Lauro based his story on forged documents created in the middle of the fifteenth century. Lauro spins a tale that states that 108 years after the great flood Noah (they lived long lives then) sailed from the mouth of the Tiber river via the Paglia river and entered the Valdichiana. He liked the fertile valley better than anywhere else in Italy (never mind that it was a swamp until the Middle Ages), so he stopped and stayed for thirty years.

Noah's son, Crano, came to the hilltop and liking the high position, the countryside, and calm air built the city of Cortona. Noah approved of Crano's work and named him king of Cortona. Crano called the kingdom Turrenia (original name of Tuscany) because Noah's descendants built cities with high towers.

Via Nazionale, the only flat street in Cortona. This is the tourist center with shops and restaurants.

ULYSSES, THE GREEKS, AND ROME

Another legend involves Ulysses and Pythagoras providing an explanation of where the Etruscans came from. Dardanus, a descendant of Noah's son Crano, fled to the Greek island of Samothrace after local disputes, and founded the city of Troy. From Troy, descendants of Dardanus, still Greek, returned to live in Turrenia (i.e. Toscana), and became the Etruscans. Among them were Ulysses and Pythagoras.

Aristotle and Theopompus (4th c. BC) reported that Ulysses emigrated to Etruria (Tuscany) to the city of Curtonaia (sounds like Cortona) after returning to Ithaca from his Odyssey. In Etruria, Ulysses was called Nanos, "the Wanderer" and his tomb is said to be at "Monte Perge" near modern Pergo a short distance east of Cortona.

According to Virgil (Aeneid III and VII), Aeneas, another descendant of Dardanus, fled the destruction of Troy and came to Latium (Lazio) where his descendants founded Rome. Hence Cortona had given rise first to Troy, and then to Rome.

BACK TO REALITY

During the fifth and fourth centuries BC, Etruscan Cortona had sophisticated political and economic systems. The Sodo excavations at the bottom of the Cortona hill have provided much information on the culture. The Etruscan walls around the city are in excellent condition with six of the original ten gates still in use, and the streets and piazzas are the same. In the third century BC Cortona and all of former Etruscan Tuscany were defeated by the Romans (who called the city Corito). The Etruscan and Roman cultures became thoroughly integrated.

Historical information after the Roman Era is sketchy until the Middle Ages when in 1150 Cortona was an independent *comune* — not under the thumb of any other town. There followed the usual intermittent periods of warfare with Arezzo, Florence, Perugia, and Siena, punctuated by brief periods of peace, however Cortona's high steep hill kept if from suffering the same violent periods as most of the other Tuscan city states. During the fifteenth century Florence took definitive control of Cortona and the rest of Tuscany and provided the stability necessary to develop its wealth and infrastructure, and to create artistic, religious, and architectural triumphs.

During WW II, on 27 June 1944, a group of German soldiers conducted a fierce retaliation in response to the killing of two of their comrades (and the wounding of a third) by Italian partisans on the 26th. Ten civilians were killed, some of them blown up with explosives after being detained in the ruins of a burned house the day before. A lieutenant of the Wehrmacht, Josef Scheungraber, was found guilty of the massacre and was subsequently sentenced to life imprisonment by a court in Munich 10 August 2009, 65 years after the massacre.

Today Cortona's economy depends chiefly on tourism with some hi-tech businesses hidden away in the buildings.

Acquacotta

Literally — Cooked Water.

Ingredients

1 medium onion, finely chopped
1 clove of garlic, minced
2 sticks of celery, finely chopped
4 carrots, finely chopped
handful of minced parsley
2 handfuls of spinach sliced into strips
3 cans of vegetable broth (or use water, but it makes a bland soup)
1/2 lb mushrooms, finely chopped
4 slices of toasted French bread

Directions

- Sauté onions, carrots, garlic, celery, mushrooms, and parsley until soft fragrant.
- Add broth and simmer for 20 minutes.
- Add the spinach and cook until soft.
- Add a slice of toast to the bottom of a bowl and ladle in some soup.
- For a variation use Swiss chard or bok choy instead of spinach.

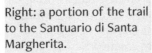
Right: a portion of the trail to the Santuario di Santa Margherita.

Below: Cortona often sits above the morning clouds floating through the Valdichiana.

Below center and bottom: Piazza Repubblica the primary piazza for locals and tourists.

Top: Monument to the fallen soldiers of Cortona during the first World War.

Above: one of the steep narrow alleys (*vicolo*) found throughout the town.

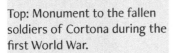

5 Piazza Repubblica and Palazzo Comunale

Location:

43.274888, 11.985475
Piazza Repubblica

Time to visit: A few minutes if in a hurry. Otherwise sit on the steps and watch your fellow tourists, or better yet, stop for lunch or *caffè* or a gelato and relax at the outdoor tables.

Reasons for a visit: It's a central location for visiting Cortona and finding your way around the confusing town.

Photography: Yes.

Accessibility: Once you get there, the piazza is as flat as any place in Cortona can be. The stairs to the Piazza Comunale are steep, but send someone ahead to the ticket office and they will provide assistance.

Piazza Repubblica, the town's main area for events and tourists.

PIAZZA REPUBBLICA

Piazza della Repubblica is the central meeting point of Cortona. From here you can get your bearings and walk any direction in the city's steep, confusing, curvy alleys and streets: Via Roma (under a vault), Via Guelfa, Via Ghibellina (covered by a vault with a bust of Pietro Berretini above the arch), Via Benedetti, Vicolo Baldelli, Vicolo Alfieri, Via Nazionale and the adjacent Piazza Signorelli meet at Piazza Repubblica.

[A *vicolo* is a narrow alleyway, often with steps leading from one street to another.]

Sitting on the steps of the Palazzo for a picture is obligatory for visitors. Restaurants line the square. The "Trattoria La Grotta," in a small alley, is one of the best places to eat in Cortona (see Chapter 19).

PALAZZO COMUNALE

Location:

Piazza della Repubblica

0575.6371

Hours:

Mon-Sat: 08.00-13.00
Free entry.

The Palazzo Comunale, city hall, existed in the first half of the twelfth century, built around a different tower.

- Over the centuries it was modified and restored as a result of fire and deterioration.
- The bells were installed in a new tower in 1530.
- Above the entrance door is the Cortona coat of arms showing St. Mark's lion.

Palazzo Comunale on Piazza Repubblica in Cortona.

- A corner of the building overlooks a sandstone column supporting the Florentine lion, *Marzocco*, symbolizing Florence's reign/control over the city (second half of the 16th c.). It is more than 500 years old but you can still read the Medicean inscription, *"Inter flores lilium, inter animalia leo"* (between the flowers, the lily, between the animals, the lion). The Cortonese considered it the symbol of St. Mark rather than of Florentine domination, which they resented.
- Inside the palace, the *Sala del Consiglio* (Town Council Hall), has an interesting coffered-ceiling and expansive stone fireplace (16th c.). The hall features restored nineteenth century paintings and decorations by Valentino Dobici. There are also allegorical figures of Justice and Peace among the portraits of favorite sons Luca Signorelli and Pietro Berrettini da Cortona.

6 Piazza Signorelli

Location:

43.275111, 11.985082
Piazza Signorelli

Time to visit: A few minutes. The most important building on the piazza is the Museo dell'Accademia Etrusca e della Città di Cortona (MAEC), one of the most important museums in Tuscany.

Reasons for a visit: Piazza Signorelli is adjacent to Piazza Repubblica and as such, another central location for visiting Cortona.

Photography: Yes.

Accessibility: Like Piazza Repubblica, it is flat.

Piazza Signorelli is next to Piazza Repubblica with two significant buildings: Palazzo Casali and Palazzo Laparelli. Palazzo Laparelli is the home of Teatro Signorelli, built in the nineteenth century.

Next to the theater is Palazzo Casali. In the twelfth century the Casali family ruled Cortona from 1325 to 1409. In 1411, the palazzo served as the seat of the Florentine government. The building was extensively remodeled in the early seventeenth century and given a higher and more imposing façade. It was remodeled again in the twentieth century to house the Museo dell'Accademia Etrusca e della Città di Cortona (MAEC).

Broccoli e Fagiolini (Broccoli and Green Beans)

Nothing fancy goes on with vegetables in Tuscany. Tuscans use fresh from the garden ingredients that they cook simply with only few seasonings for subtle flavor.

Ingredients

1 head of broccoli cut into its florets
1/2 lb green beans trimmed
2 cloves of garlic, minced
4 T EVOO
red pepper flakes to taste
salt and pepper

Directions

- Place broccoli into a pot of water and boil about 4 minutes until just *al dente*. Plunge florets into ice water to stop further cooking.
- Cook the green beans the same way, about 8 minutes. Cool in ice water.
- Heat olive oil in a broad shallow pan.
- Drain beans and broccoli in a colander.
- Add beans and broccoli to the pan and sauté with garlic until hot and tender.
- Sprinkle with pepper flakes, season with salt and pepper, and serve.

7 MAEC

Museo dell'Accademic Etrusca e della Città

Location:

43.275111, 11.985082
Palazzo Casali
Piazza Signorelli 9

0575.630415

Website: http://www.cortonamaec.org/english/index.php

Email:

info@cortonamaec.org

Reservations:

prenotazioni@cortona-maec.org

Telephone: 0575.630415
Fax: 0575.637.248

About €7.00. You can make reservations online, though I've never found it necessary.
€13.00 combination ticket for MAEC and Museo Diocesano. Ask at the counter.

Hours:

Apr through Oct: everyday: 10:00-19:00
Nov through Mar: Tues-Sun: 10.00-17.00, closed Mon.
Closed Christmas.

Time to visit: About two hours.

Reasons for a visit: The Museo dell'Accademic Etrusca e della Città is a beautiful museum, modern in every way with large displays, reconstructions and dioramas to give a context for the finds. It has video kiosks for more information. Mostly Etruscan artifacts with some art from the Renaissance through eighteenth

A piece of Attic pottery like the collection in MAEC. (WMC, Codex)

Bucchero pottery in the MAEC. (WMC, Sailko)

century. There are also a few tactile displays. The *Lampadario Etrusco* and *Tempietto Ginori* are the prizes of the collection.

Photography: Yes. No flash, no supports, no selfie sticks.

Accessibility: Very good. Elevators, mini-lifts, and ramps. Still, there are a couple of minor areas not accessible.

HIGHLIGHTS

The Museum was founded in 1727 with the collections and library of Onofrio Baldelli. The collections sprawl through four floors: the lower level focuses on Etruscan and Roman times; the upper floors display artistic elements from the Etruscan through twentieth centuries including furnishings, cinerary urns, and modern art. The museum is also conducting an excavation of an Etruscan temple at the Sodo site at the bottom of the Cortona hill.

There are two paths to follow through the museum: the most logical begins with Etruscan and Roman eras on the below ground level and proceeds through the top level; or you can begin from the twentieth century at the top and work your way to the lower level. Either way I get lost and have to do some backtracking.

Unfortunately there is no audio tour, which a place this large and important should have. Many of the display signs have English versions, but not all.

FINDING YOUR WAY

Note: I struggle on a yearly basis to keep this chapter accurate. While the lower floor and Etruscan and Roman exhibits seldom change, the upper floors change every year. This chapter represents my most current visit: October 2019.

What follows are some of the more important objects to find. The rooms are sequentially numbered, just follow the arrows. Sometimes you may have to walk out of a room and return the way you came to find the entrance to the next room. In some rooms, the lights brighten automatically when you enter.

Bronze tools. Room 2.

I begin the tour by leaving the ticket desk and going down the stairs after a brief look at a Paleolithic display. Near the bottom of the stairs is a toilet — keep it in mind.

ROOM 1: PALEONTOLOGY

- Room 1 is the first area (small and uninteresting) after the ticket/bookstore displaying fossils from the Paleolithic Era with a beautiful diorama background.

ROOM 2: PREHISTORY AND EARLY SETTLEMENT

Walk down the steps to the lower level.

- Room 2 houses materials from early settlements in the prehistoric period. There are materials from the Stone through the Bronze and Iron Ages found around Cortona including terracotta vases and bowls.
- There is a polychrome funerary urn here.
- There is reconstruction of a hut from the earliest Etruscan time, the ninth century BC.
- The cabinets display objects of everyday life.

ROOM 3: HISTORY OF ETRUSCAN SETTLEMENTS

Artifacts from Etruscan and Roman eras.

- The wall illustration shows the reconstruction of ancient Roman roads throughout Tuscany.

Bucchero Pottery

Etruscan pottery from the pre-Roman period, about the seventh through early fifth centuries BC. Characteristically black and shiny from polishing.

Attic Pottery

A red and black type of pottery with origins to ancient Greece.

Etruscan skeleton, about 6th century BC. *Room 4.*

- There is a model of the tumulus of the Sodo excavation at the bottom of the Cortona hill.
- An illustration also shows the locations of major archaeological sites.

ROOM 4: ANCIENT CORTONA AND SODO EXCAVATIONS

- Room 4 displays many of the objects from the Sodo excavations.
- One of the finds in the Sodo excavations is a large altar. There is a mockup of the altar here. The altar, from the sixth century, is upon a platform six steps high.
- The shiny black bucchero pottery is reminiscent of the pottery made by the Pueblo Native Americans.
- There is a large fossilized skeleton of a tall Etruscan with a small jug; very few Etruscan remains have been found.
- A number of funeral urns are displayed. Objects found in the urns include burnt bones, personal items like bronze fibulae and pendants, iron fibulae, clothing ornaments, bronze braid holders, amber and vitreous paste beads, and pendants. The objects show direct trade links with people in the Po Valley, Umbria, and Latium.
- These rooms also show sophisticated Etruscan artifacts including jewelry, attic pottery, everyday house objects, and bronzes.

ROOM 5: SERGARDI COLLECTION

- Room 5 is a small room about half way up a ramp. It contains more artifacts from the museum's excavations.
- The Sergardi collection displays attic, bucchero, and terracotta pottery.

ROOMS 6: ANCIENT CORTONA AND THE CAMUCIA EXCAVATION

Room 6 is up a few steps from Room 5. It includes objects from the tumulus found in Camucia, a small town at the bottom of the Cortona hill.

- Ivory artifacts and more Attic pottery from local Etruscan tombs. Excavations of these sites is ongoing.
- There is a "mourners' slab" made up of three tufa blocs that once adorned a luxurious funerary bed with eight carved kneeling female figures performing acts of grief. The two central figures are covering their faces while the others beat their breasts (second half of 6th c. BC).
- There are more objects from the Sergardi pottery collection.

ROOM 7: THE CAMUCIA EXCAVATION

- The diagrams show the Sphere of Influence of Cortona in the Iron Age.
- More cinerary urns.
- Helmets and axes for war.
- A small terracotta of a kneeling horse where the rider is missing.

Mourners' Slab" for funerary bed. Room 6.

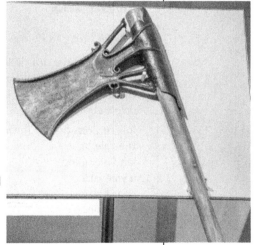

Large battle axe in Room 7.

- Objects include jewelry, gold leaf diadems from the necropolis at the Chiesa di San Francesco in Foiano, rings, cups, knives, helmets, axes, banquet items, and swords.

Etruscan funerary urn in Room 9. The top carving represents the deceased while the carving on the side depicts bravery in a battle.

ROOM 8: EXCAVATION AT PORTA BIFORA

Go back through rooms 6 and 7 to find Room 8.

- Porta Bifora is an ancient gate through the Etruscan wall.
- Model of statues that can be held by a blind person.
- There are a number of architectural artifacts and finely made large kettles here.

ROOM 9: ETRUSCAN FUNERARY URNS

- There are three urns in Room 9. The top carving depicts the deceased. The side carvings are often battle scenes displaying the deceased's bravery. Sometimes the side is carved with a celebration.
- Inscriptions on the *Tabula Cortenesis,* bronze sheets recording the sale of land including a vineyard near Lake Trasimeno. The *tabula* was found in 1992.

Roman mosaic from Villa Osaia in Room 14.

ROOM 10: FROM ETRUSCAN TO ROMAN CORTONA

- There is a large black and white mosaic from the floor of

Cortona's Le Piazza Tomasi Roman public baths.

ROOM 11: THE VILLA OSAIA

- There are models of a Roman villa at Ossaia during the Roman Imperial period around the fifth century.
- A mosaic floor in black and white tiles.
- More objects from Etruscan tombs including nails, bowls, vases, ivory needles, small sculptures.

ROOM 12: VILLA OSAIA AND THE GLIRARIUM

- Many of the objects are terracotta amphorae. The large jars are examples of luxury items and used for storing food and wine.
- Unique is a *glirarium*, a large amphora with air holes all around used to raise dormice, a Roman delicacy. Dormice are tiny (2.4 to 7-inches long) rodents with furred rather than scaly tails. In Roman times, they were raised in captivity, fattened, stuffed, and served as a delicacy or snack.

Glirarium used for raising dormice, a Roman delicacy.

ROOM 13 AND 14: MORE FROM VILLA OSAIA

- More terracotta.
- Terracotta oil lamps.
- Geometric mosaic floors from Roman villas in the Augustinian Age and third century BC.

Ancient Roman Dormice Recipe

Pound the dormouse meat with pepper and place in an earthenware bowl with caraway, cumin, bay leaves, dates, honey, vinegar, wine, and olive oil and then roast them in an oven. (I don't know if they skin them first or eat the fur.) They are still eaten today in Slovenia.

MAEC ROOMS AE

[Important notes about rooms AE.]

First, rooms AE cover a wide time period and huge range of subjects. They are located on two floors and a small mezzanine. Take the staircase or elevator to the first floor to begin. The collections include Tuscan painting, eighteenth century furnishings, coins, medals, pottery, additional Etruscan artifacts, Egyptian objects, the Gino Severini room, and the prize of the Museum's collection, the Etruscan *lampadario*.

The Croce Viaria in a glass case in Room AE4, the Sala del Medioevo Cortonese.

Second, the rooms do not follow in logical order.

Third, the exhibits in these rooms seem to get reorganized frequently. The following description is based on a fall 2019 visit to the MAEC. It is a confusing warren of rooms and hallways. The logical progression does not follow the numbers consecutively.

EGYTIAN ROOMS

After finishing with the lower level Etruscan and Roman exhibits there is a steep stairway to the first floor (elevator nearby).

When you reach the first floor you will find two rooms with artifacts from early Egypt including scupltures, fabrics, statuettes, sarcophagi and mummies.

> **A Mythology Lesson: The Satyrs**
>
> In Greek mythology, the satyr was a companion and teacher to wine god Dionysius. Satyrs resemble a man of the forest with ears and body of a horse. Later he was portrayed as a bald fat man with thick lips and a squat nose with human legs. When drunk, the satyr was said to have special knowledge and the power of prophecy.
>
> **Sirens**
>
> Three dangerous winged women seductresses who lured sailors with their enchanting music to shipwreck on the rocky coast of their island.

- Another valuable symbol of the museum is a small stucco and wood *Funeral Boat* from a tomb in a glass case.
- The second room displays papyrus and hieroglyphic texts. In the center are two sarcophagi (4th c. BC) and two mummies. The wall cabinets hold objects of everyday use

Find another set of steps to the second floor to find the Sala del Medioevo Cortonese.

AE4: SALA DEL MEDIOEVO CORTONESE

- This room at the top of the stairs has several religous paintings and parts of triptychs.
- In a glass case is the well-carved *Croce Viaria* (12th c.) with several religious symbols.
- On the wall is a deceptive mosaic, the *Madonna Orante* (13th c.). Deceptive because it looks like a modern art version of the Madonna and not 700 years old.
- A glass case with coins and medallions.
- One of the triptychs is by Bicci di Lorenzo (15th c.) with the *Madonna and Child between a Bishop, John the Baptist, Michael the Archangel, and Saint Catherine of Alexandria.*

Above: Madonna Orante, Madonna Praying, Room AE4.

AE5: SALA DEL LAMPADARIO ETRUSCO

The most valuable piece in the museum hangs here, the Etruscan *lampadario*, or chandelier (late 5th BC). The solid bronze object (132 pounds) was discovered near Cortona in 1840. The Etruscan Academy had to pay 1600 Florentine *scudi* (about $225,000 today) to acquire it. The original hangs from the ceiling and a model sits in a lighted niche in the wall.

- The carving is a bas-relief about 14-inches in diameter.

Below: the Etruscan chandelier, room AE5.

Two small statues of Roman wrestlers in the Sala del Biccione, AE3.

- Under the 18 burners for candles along the outside ring are alternating figures of sirens and satyrs. The sirens have arms resting on their chests, and are wearing a tunic with a double chain wound in the hair. The satyrs are playing panpipes and have erections.
- The next ring depicts leaping dolphins on stylized waves.
- Next are wild animal hunts.
- Finally, in the center is a gargoyle with an open mouth, fangs, and tongue hanging out. Around it are curled snakes.
- Between each nozzle is a horned head of Achelous, god of the Achelous river, the largest in Greece.

AE3: SALA DEL BICCIONE

A ramp leads down to Room AE3, the largest in the museum. Not everything here is labeled. There is *a lot* of stuff here and it would

Etruscan cinerary urns at the entrance to the Sala del Biccione, AE3.

be easy to spend an hour wandering around the cases. In here you will find . . .

- More Etruscan stone funerary urns.
- Paintings from the Gothic Era to the Renaissance to the eighteenth century.
- The room includes two rows of glass cases with Etruscan, Hellenistic, and Roman objects. These include small statuettes, ex votos, personal objects, and attic and bucchero pottery. There are many fertility statuettes of women with large breasts and men with erections. Some figures represent *Culsans*, the god of doors and doorways, and *Silvans*, the god of boundaries.
- There are a number of terracotta statuettes depicting children in swaddling clothes belonging to an Etruscan place of worship and linked to fertility.
- Everyday objects include ceramics, glass, ointment jars, pots, a cheese grater, mirrors, broaches, and a group of oil lamps.
- Artifacts from Roman times include architectural decoration fragments, votive bronzes, ointment jars, lamps, and figurines. There are terracotta figurines and body parts that served as *ex votos* offered to health-related deities.
- A tondo of the *Madonna and Child with Saints* that are protectors of Cortona (Luca Signorelli, 1512). Among them is Michael the Archangel and Santa Margherita (behind the baby). The painting borrows symbolism from the concept of the Immaculate Conception: Mary supported by the heads of cherubs as Mary crushes Satan, representing her role in the doctrine of salvation.
- A small picture of the *Adoration of the Shepherds* (Luca Signorelli, early 16th c.). The baby Christ is laying on the floor in the stable, his head and back supported by a bundle of straw. As Signorelli often did, there is more of the story in the background showing an Angel announcing Christ's presence

The Adoration of the Shepherds by Signorelli in the Sala del Biccione, AE3.

The top two pieces depict four saints and two angels.
Bottom piece: Saints Philip, Reparata Virgin, Matthew, Tecla Virgin, Paul, Anastasia Virgin, Lawrence, ?, ?.

to the shepherds. Elements of this painting are seen in a larger painting in the Cortona Museo Diocesano.

- A painting of the *Resurrection* by Santo di Tito (16th c.).
- There are six sets of predellas that were once part of larger altarpieces. These predellas portray saints.
- A large painting by Pietro Berrettini depicts the *Madonna with Baby and Saints* (1628). John the Baptist is on the Madonna's right and St. Francis on her left.
- Most significant is a Christian glass cup with a monogram and inscription from the fourth century.
- Red figured Tyrrhenian amphora depicting Hercules's first of ten labors, *Hercules and the Nemean Lion*.
- Bucchero ware is sometimes considered the "national" pottery of Etruria. Here there is typical Etruscan pottery used for both funerary rites and everyday use. Artifacts include miniature statues, goblets, amphorae, wine jugs, and others. The black color comes from clay fired in kilns with no oxygen. Some pieces are braziers from Chiusi used for funerary purposes. Two pieces contain miniaturized vases and utensils for tombs.
- Altar piece of the *Virgin with Child with Saints Francis, Pope Stephen, John the Baptist, and James* (Pietro Berrettini da Cortona, 17th c.).
- *Madonna and Child with young John the Baptist* (Pinturicchio, 15th c.).
- *Miracle of the Wine* (Baccio Ciarpi, 16th to 17th c.).

AE6: GALLERIA

This is a small hallway off Sala del Biccione.

- Most interesting are the large ancient globes under protective plexiglass. Look at the features of the continents — what was known at that time. They were done by Moroncelli in 1710.
- On the wall is a simplified Medici coat of arms with only the six "pills" representing their first profession as doctors, *medici*.

Chess and checkers set in the Tomassi rooms AE7-AE9.

[NO NUMBER]: SALA PIAZZETTA

This is a small room off the *Galleria* without a number. It leads to AE7.

The Severini room holds a range of materials providing an insight into his artistic interests throughout his life including futurism, cubism, realism, and mixed media. The donation, made official by the widow and daughters after his death, was further enriched by other works from his family and Alfonso Leonetti, a famous Cortonese intellectual.

- *Maternità* — Motherhood (1916). One of his most famous works portraying his wife, Jeanne Fort, nursing their newborn son, Antonio.
- The lithographs show his marvelous use of color and composition.
- An early work is the fascinating *Bohémienne* (1905) reflecting the exciting artistic atmosphere of early twentieth century Paris.
- Two mixed media pieces from 1964 are part of a series called the *Industrial Age*.

The Maternità by Cortona artist Gino Severini.

Coat and person-carrier in the Tomassi rooms, AE7-AE9.

- *Parisian Woman*, 1906.
- Sketches.
- Collection of paintings from his cubist period.

AE7, AE8, AND AE9: SALE DEI TOMASSI

The family Tommasi were patrons of the museum through several generations. The following sequence of bullets follows roughly the path through the rooms.

- Ceramic writing tools: ink pot, pens, and sand shaker.
- Tommasi family portraits from the seventeenth century are on the walls.
- A small hallway has a beautiful model ship: a merchant vessel with tiny pulleys, oars, sails, and rudder.
- An eighteenth century commode.
- Many precious stones made in Florence.
- Giovanni Battista Tommasi's richly decorated bedroom is furnished with eighteenth century furniture including a huge canopy bed with crests of the family, gilded wood, large mirror, and portrait of the Grand Maestro of Malta.
- In the corridor are engravings, miniatures, and finely carved ivory objects including a Cantonese (1756) chess and checker set with exquisitely carved pieces. There is another game with a tiny cup and even tinier dice.
- Above the game shelf is another game with more intricate carvings.
- Rooms have items of every day use including votive candles, oil candles, and plates.
- Swords and dueling pistols.
- A carrier for one person.
- A chandelier of Murano glass from Venice.
- Medieval paintings and examples of clothing are scattered about.

AE15: ACCADEMIA ETRUSCO

This large meeting room was once the city court room. It has a large emblem of the Grand Duke Ferdinand II in the center of the wooden ceiling. On the walls of the hall are a series of portraits of Medici and prominent Cortonese.

AE12: SALA GINORI

The room has valuable documents about the history of Etruria and the porcelain *Tempietto Ginori*.

- The *Tempietto Ginori* is another of the most precious objects in the MAEC collection. The shiny, pristine, impossibly delicate looking porcelain is the Rococo *Tempietto*, donated by Carlo Ginori (1756). It stands in the center of the room, roped off for protection. (Out for restoration fall 2017.)
  - The blue and white porcelain temple was made in Florence and celebrates the Medici family.
  - Mercury tops the temple.
  - It is decorated with allegorical figures on both sides of the winged god, Mercury.
  - The figures in the center represent Beauty kidnapped by Time.
  - The lower part depicts Fortitude, Prudence, Concordia, and Purity.
  - There are 76 portrait medallions of the Medici family.
- Along the walls and on tables of the room are precious gems, coins, rings, and gold.

AE1: SALA VENTURI

- Architectural elements.
- Carvings.
- Display cases (empty in 2017).

The Tempietto Ginori in AE12, Sala Ginori. (Photo from MAEC)

Musa Polimnia, AE2, Sala Baldelli.

AE2: SALA BALDELLI

Onofrio Baldelli was a major contributor to starting the Etruscan Accademia. These rooms display portraits of the museum founders and a collection of inscriptions on stone, bronze figurines, coins, urns, and statues.

- Another of the most valuable paintings is the *Musa Polimnia* (16th-18th c.), (see next page) the Greek Muse of sacred song, oratory, and lyric poetry, painted on slate. She wears an exquisite diaphanous covering and poses with a barely noticeable "come hither" grin. The painting is "encaustic," that is, it was made with pigments mixed with hot wax and then burned into the slate.

Full suit of armor in the Armory, Sala degli Armi.

- Along the walls are more cinerary urns including five made of Volterra alabaster with Hellenistic themes.
- Statues of Tinia and the Goddess Aritimi.

SALA DEGLI ARMI

- The armory room has a collection of ceremonial weapons, armor, and a high quality chest with wrought iron folding mechanism. There is a full suit of armor standing erects.

- Other artifacts include lances, helmets, chest guards, and a large collection of pistols, rifles, and crossbows.

BIBLIOTECA

- The antiquarian library holds over 10,000 books providing information about the development of western Europe on shelves at least fifteen-feet high.
- The library was begun in 1797, but holds documents from before the sixteenth century including works of parchment, manuscripts, incunabula (books printed before 1501), and paper codes.
- Valuable is a manuscript of the *Divine Comedy* by Dante Alighieri and a thirteenth century book of common prayer with lyrics and music.
- Furniture dates back to the eighteenth century.

Top: Mosaics in the MAEC.
Above: The MAEC Egyptian mummies.

8 Melone il Sodo Excavation

AKA: Il Parco Archeologico

Attention: Though hours are scheduled it seems to be staffed in a casual manner. Someone may be there, or not.

Location:

43.28128, 11.96729
Loc. Sodo di Cortona
Località il Molino

0575.637235

The tumulus of the Melone il Sodo excavation.

Ask at the MAEC for directions. At the bottom of the Cortona hill, before turning to follow the road up to the top, is a small dirt track to an active excavation about 200 meters from the main road.

Hours: They seem to be irregular, but mid morning is your best chance. The caretaker comes and goes on a whim. Also, check the website. Officially, in August 2019, the hours were:

Daily: 10.00-14.00, 15.00-18.00

Website: https://cortonamaec.org/it/il-parco-archeologico/

Email: info@cortonamaec.org

Information: http://www.en.cortonaguide.com/melone_ii.html

Accessibility: Flat but difficult as it is dirt, grass, and gravel around the tumulus.

The first time I saw this dig was in 2000 not long after it had begun. Visible then were only the temple steps leading to the altar. Today the excavation has expanded to opening the interior and outside of the temple revealing some foundation stones of buildings a few meters to the side.

The Melone II of Sodo is at the base of the Cortona hill on the north bank of the Rio di Loreto, a canal. There are two separate inner tombs on the west side: Tomb I, excavated in 1928-29, consists of two separate inner tombs dug into the tumulus. Sarcophagi and funereal urns along with over 100 pieces of necklaces, beads, pendants, earrings, and rings are on display at

At the Melone Sodo excavation and tombs: steps leading to a sacrificial altar; the interior of a tomb.

the MAEC. Of particular note in the MAEC are corbels and other bronze elements posed on small stools; a stylus showing the mastery of writing skills by Etruscans and black glazed Attic pottery and weapons.

Tomb II was discovered in 1991 and contained a wealth of gold artifacts. It had been pillaged in ancient times, but much was still preserved by the collapse of part of the stone and dirt roof of the mound. Artifacts date from the fifth to the second centuries BC. Excavations exposed a large altar platform on the east side whose sidewalls are decorated with reliefs and sculptures depicting a battle between a warrior trying to kill a lioness who is trying to bite off his head.

During the Roman period the tombs fell in disuse and the tumulus became overgrown with vegetation, camouflaging its original purpose. However the area retained a funerary function with single burials around the altar. Many blocks from the altar were taken and reused.

9 Museo Diocesano — Diocesan Museum

Location:

43.276370, 11.983919

Piazza del Duomo 1
0575-62830

Website: http://www.diocesiarezzo.it/index.php?option=com_content&view=article&id=447&Itemid=253

Website: http://www.cortonaweb.net/en/history/21-cortona-diocesan-museum

Email: museodiocesano.cortona@diocesi.arezzo.it

Hours:

1 April to 31 October:
Daily 10.00-18.30

1 November to 31 March:
Tues-Sun 10.00-17.00

About €5.00.

Time to visit: One hour with audio. Two pleasant hours with careful appreciation. This small museum avoids mediocrity. Everything is worth studying.

Reasons for a visit: If you visit but one place in Cortona, this should be it. It has a small but fantastic collection of art from the Middle Ages through the twentieth century — here you don't have to wade through a bunch of mediocrity to find the masters. Hall 4, the Signorelli room, is worth twice the cost of admission. I highly recommend the audio tour, it's one of the best that I've used — concise and informative.

Photography: No.

Accessibility: Partially accessible on first floor. The lower level is accessible only by a long narrow stairway.

HIGHLIGHTS

The Diocesan Museum, established in 1948, is in the former Chiesa di Gesù. The Church of Gesù was built between 1498 and 1505 and

The Sarcophagus decorated with the Battle Between the Amazons and Dionysius. Sala 1.

was made up of an oratory on the lower floor and a church with a single nave and three altars on the upper floor.

The collection includes most of the valuable works of art coming from important churches in Cortona and the surrounding area. The paintings are from the Middle Ages through the Renaissance including works from Niccolò di Segna, Pietro Lorenzetti, Luca Signorelli, and Bartolomeo della Gatta. Perhaps the most important work is the *Annunciation* by Fra Angelico.

SALA 1: HALL OF THE SARCOPHAGI

Sala 2. Detail from Pietro Lorenzetti's Enthroned Madonna Gazing at the Child.

- The exhibition begins with an ancient, well preserved marble Roman sarcophagus (2nd c.) in the Hellenistic style decorated with the *Battle between the Amazons and Dionysius*. The work was discovered in the fifteenth century buried in a nearby field beneath the city walls. The sarcophagus was admired by Donatello and Brunelleschi, who came to Cortona to view it.

- The battle was in front of the walls of Ephesus, Turkey.
- Dionysius is on the left with a crown of vine leaves.
- On the right end is a chariot driven by a winged woman led by two centaurs. A man wearing oriental clothes is unsaddled by an opponent who holds the horse by the bit in front of the gates of Ephesus.
- In the center are battle scenes.

- On the left wall are two angels sculpted in marble (14th c.).
- Above the door to the next room is a fresco of *Madonna with Child*.

> **Franciscans of the Third Order**
>
> The Third Order consists of men and women, single or in committed relationships, who, though following ordinary professions, are called to a dedicated life of service to our Lord through prayer, study, and work. Tertiaries follow Francis in prayer and action by striving to be peacemakers, working for social justice, and deepening their relationship with God. They share Francis's concerns for the well-being of the earth, the poor, and the marginalized. (Source: http://tssf.org)

SALA 2: OLD SACRISTY AND THE SENESE COLLECTION

The old sacristy is behind Hall 3, a little illogical since you enter Hall 3 first. These are works of artists from Siena in the fourteenth century and the Basilica of Santa Margherita.

- A painting on wood of the *Enthroned Madonna Gazing at the Child with Four Angels* (Lorenzetti, 1320). Note the flat features, lack of perspective, elongated fingers, and slanted eyes, all typical of the twelfth through fourteenth century Gothic paintings. The gaze between Mary and Christ is intense, as if communicating mentally. The script at the bottom is a bit of immodesty by the painter, "Pietro di Lorenzo, a Senese, painted it with skill."
- Another work of the Senese school is the painting to the right, *Virgin with Child* (Niccolò di Segna, 1336). Note the fingers and the length of baby Jesus's toes. The surrounding gold represents eternity, sanctity, and the supernatural. Christ has an adult and angry look on his face while Mary looks out in a dreamlike state.
- The most important work here is the tempera painting on wood of the *History of St. Margaret of Cortona* (Margheritone d'Arezzo, 1298), the patron saint of Cortona. The painting is over 700 years old and is in poor condition.
  - Margaret stands dressed in a checkered dress covered by a dark cloak. She holds a rosary in her left hand and her right

The history of Santa Magherita in Sala 2. (WGA)

hand is on her breast.
- The bare feet are given an unnatural prominence to underscore her profound repentance.

Around her are eight events of her life, difficult to decipher because of the condition of the painting:

- Left, top down:
  - Margaret knocks at the door of St. Francis's convent while two friars consult one another.

The Annuciation by Fra Angelico, 1443 in Museo Diocesano di Cortona. Sala 2. (WGA)

- She receives the habit of a Franciscan of the Third Order.
- She distributes bread to the poor.
- She saves a man who had hanged himself.
- On the right, top down:
  - She may be washing the feet of lepers.
  - Christ by intercession of St. Francis forgives Margaret's sins. She was a mistress of married mens.
  - In her cell she receives communion from a friar.
  - Christ and the Madonna show Margaret her throne in heaven.
- Below, Margaret is dead in her catafalque.
- Two marble sculptures from the early fourteenth century of *Virgins with Child* (Senese school, 1305). The one on the left is better preserved and attributed to Giano di Fazio.
- There are four fresco fragments from the ancient church of St. Margaret (1334). Two represent *Christ Bearing the Cross*. Christ's face reflects the physical and mental fatigue of his suffering. A fifth fragment is called the *Head of an Apostle*.

Detail from the Annunciation providing some of the backstory: An angel sends Adam and Eve from Paradise. (WMC, the Yorck Project)

SALA 3: THE OLD CHURCH OF GESÙ

This is the former nave of the old Church of Jesus.

- Above the center altar is a painting of the *Annunciation* by Beato (Fra) Angelico (1436). It was commissioned by a cloth merchant for the Church of San Domenico.
  - The angel and Mary wear garments embroidered with gold. They sit under an arcade and outside is a detailed flower garden.
  - In the upper left corner is an example of a "backstory," a small scene showing Adam and Eve leaving the security of the Garden of Eden after eating the forbidden fruit. This small piece is a counter play to the Annunciation, which is about the salvation of humankind whereas the sin of Adam and Eve condemned man.
  - Gabriel's speech comes out of his mouth in a ribbon saying, "The Holy Ghost shall come upon thee and the power of the Highest shall overshadow thee."

Pietro Lorenzetti's Crucifixion in Sala 3.

- Mary's response, partly covered by a column, says, "Behold the handmaid of the Lord; be it unto me according to thy word."
- The predella is composed of scenes from the life of the Virgin, from left to right:
  - The Virgin's Birth.
  - Marriage of the Virgin.
  - The Visitation to St. Elizabeth. Note the beauty of the land-scape, a view from Cortona in the 1400s.
  - Adoration of the Magi.
  - Presentation of Jesus at the Temple.
  - Death of the Virgin.
  - The Virgin gives the Habit to St. Dominic.
- Below Angelico's painting is a *Baptismal Font* sculpted from marble (Ciuccio di Nuccio, 1474). The front relief depicts the baptism of Christ.
- A triptych of the *Enthroned Virgin With Child between John the Evangelist, John the Baptist, Matthew, and Mary Magdalen* (Fra Angelico, 1437). The two side tondos represent the Annunciation and at the center is the Crucifixion. The predella has images from the life of St. Dominic and other saints:
  - St. Peter Martyr.
  - Innocent III's dream of St. Dominic holding up the falling church.
  - Meeting between St. Dominic and St. Francis.

- St. Dominic receives the book and the stick from the apostles Peter and Paul.
- St. Michael the Archangel.
- Healing of Napoleone Orsini.
- Dispute of St. Dominic.
- St. Vincent (?).
- The Angels serve dinner to the friars.
- Death of St. Dominic.
- St. Thomas Aquinas.

Fran Angelico's triptych altarpiece, 1437, in Sala 3.

- On the side wall is a triptych of the *Madonna and Child with Saints Nicholas, Michael the Archangel, John the Baptist, and Margaret of Hungary* (Sassetta, 1435). The left and right tondos show the Annunciation and the center shows Agnus Dei (Lamb of God).
- Above a small side altar is the *Crucifixion* (Pietro Lorenzetti, 1320). Though typically Gothic with elongated limbs and a head looking down by attaching an angled piece of wood, it is a powerful depiction of His death with blood everywhere and the inconsolable sorrow of Mary and St. John. The star-shaped top of the cross shows the Risen Christ.
- A polyptych with *Three Franciscan Saints* (Domenico di Michelino, 1470) on a gold background: St. Francis, St. Bernardino of Siena, and St. Anthony of Padua.
- *Assumption of the Virgin* (Martino di Bartolomeo, 1408). The artist probably used a young Tuscan girl as a model, there is much more detail in the face than some paintings that depict Mary in a sort of abstract and flat manner. She sits upon her throne in a regal posture looking like the Queen she is.
- *Assumption* where *Mary gives St. Thomas Her Belt* (Bartolomeo della Gatta, 1475). Many paintings of the Assumption show Mary handing her belt to St. Thomas (ever the doubter) to prove that it is she who has gone to heaven. Mary's arrival in heaven is celebrated by angels singing and playing instruments.

Below, the twelve apostles stand around Mary's tomb, shocked, while Thomas looks up to heaven. The apostles look old and tired.

> **Workshop of...**
> "From the studio of" or "workshop of" refer to paintings that were probably started by the master with sketches and some basic painting, but then finished by his apprentices.

- The intricate ceiling is carved and painted wood by local master Mezzanotte (1536). It was restored in 1985. There are 45 octagonal pieces and 32 small squares, all with carved relief decorations, painted, and gilded including wild animals, flowers, pine cones, and fruit. Other shapes symbolize the Passion of Christ and sacred texts.

SIGNORELLI 4: SIGNORELLI COLLECTION

This is the greatest room in the museum. It's possible to stand and look at any one of these grand paintings for an hour — or a day. Luca Signorelli is one of Cortona's — and the world's — most distinguished artists.

Signorelli's Campianto, Lamentation Over the Dead Christ, in Sala 4.

9 Museo Diocesano — Diocesan Museum

- The *Campianto sul Christo Morto* (Lamentation Over the Dead Christ, 1502). In 1502, Signorelli returned to Cortona from Rome where his first born died of the Black Plague and another son was killed in a brawl. He painted the *Compianto* as an expression of his grief using the image of his son as the model for Christ. This is one of the most expressive paintings you will ever see. It's packed with stories:
  - In the foreground is the main topic, Christ's body on Mary's lap and His legs on Mary Magdalen's lap.
  - A hammer and skull (symbol of Golgotha) sit below the cross.
  - St. John stands above the women, blood from Christ's feet staining the cross above his head. To the right of St. John is another saint (possibly St. Peter) holding the nails and crown of thorns.
  - On the left in the background is a scene of the crucifixion with Christ between two criminals, a vast crowd of people below, many of them Roman soldiers.
  - On the right is Christ's resurrection as he leaves the tomb.

> **Luca Signorelli**
>
> Born Luca d'Egidio di Ventura in Cortona between 1441 and 1445. He was 82 when he died and is buried in Cortona in the Church of San Francesco, but the location of his tomb is unknown.
>
> In 1472, he began painting in Arezzo as an apprentice. He painted mostly sacred pictures and frescoes, mostly in Tuscany but also in Rome. There is a single fresco of his in the Sistine Chapel, the *Acts of Moses*. After painting scenes from the life of St. Benedict, he went to Orvieto and painted a series of massive frescoes of the *Last Judgment* and the *Resurrection of the Flesh* in the Duomo. Michelangelo is said to have borrowed from Signorelli's ideas for his *Last Judgment* in the Sistine Chapel.
>
> He was one of the first great artists to master perspective and the art of foreshortening. He paid attention to anatomy and is said to have studied corpses (stolen from burial grounds). He was a master of detail and usually included several stories in one painting.
>
> By 1499 he had works all over Tuscany and in the Vatican. Simply, he is one of the greatest from the Valdichiana and Tuscany.

Detail from Signorelli's Campianto. Sala 4.

Sala 4. Christ giving communion to the Apostles. (WGA)

- In the center is an ideal Tuscan landscape, interrupted by the blood on the cross.
- Now look at the predella, there are scenes of the *Passion of Christ*:
    - The Agony of Christ in the Garden of Gethsemane.
    - The Last Supper.
    - The center of the predella is a chalice with a communion host.
    - Christ Captured at Gethsemane.
    - The Flagellation. Five Roman soldiers are beating Christ.
- Signorelli painted the *Communion of the Apostles* in 1512. The apostles, some standing, some on their knees, surround Christ to receive the consecrated Host. Judas leans to one side hiding the Host in his purse with a guilty look thinking of his upcoming betrayal.
- The *Virgin with Child and Saints Frances, Lodovico of Tolosa, Bonaventura of Bagnoreggio, and Saint Anthony of Padua* (Signorelli, 1515). Note the fine details in the clothing and

expressions and Christ's gaze upon St. Francis who is shown with his stigmata.

- *Virgin with Child and Saints Michael, Antonio da Padova, Bernardino di Siena, and Nicholas di Bari* (Workshop of Signorelli, 1515). The characters stand on two levels defined by a pedestal. In the background is a solid blue sky. Sant'Antonio holds his tongue, which is now on display in the Basilica di Sant'Antonio in Padova.
- Stories from the *Life of St. Benedict* (Workshop of Signorelli, 1516). The subjects echo his frescoes in the Abbazia Monte Oliveto Maggiore:
  - St. Benedict Orders Friar Mauaro to walk on water to save Friar Placido from drowning.
  - A friar is killed in a fall after the devil pushed him off a wall.
  - St. Benedict revives the friar who fell from the wall.
  - He throws himself into the bushes to defeat temptations.
  - He retires into the cave and is fed by Romano who lets down the food with a rope.
- *Assumption of the Virgin* (Workshop of Signorelli, 1520). Mary is led to heaven by choirs of angels while the apostles look to her tomb in amazement.
- *Nativity* (Workshop of Signorelli, 1521). The tiny Child lays upon a small cloth in front of the Shepherds while choirs of angels sing. Old St. Joseph and Mary adore the Child. In the background, left, the shepherds are receiving word of Christ's birth from the angels. In the MAEC, there is a much smaller version of this painting, probably a test painting.
- *Presentation of Jesus at the Temple* (Workshop of Signorelli, 1521). The rabbi holds the fragile looking Christ with Mary on the other side. Many people stand around looking inquisitive. The predella includes scenes from a miracle by St. Anthony: the Miracle of Bolsena. At the ends are St. Francis and St. Anthony.

Sala 4. The Assumption by Signorelli.

Sala 4. Detail from Luca and Francesco Signorelli's Allegory of the Immaculate Conception.

- *Adoration of the Shepherds* (Workshop of Signorelli, 1522). Note the landscape with its frame of rocky outcroppings. On the left of the outcropping the angels are telling the shepherds of Christ's birth.
- *Allegory of the Immaculate Conception* (Luca and Francesco Signorelli, 1523, Francesco is the nephew of Luca). At the top is God surrounded by angels. Mary is the largest character looking a little paunchy. Mary is standing on the tree of life from which Adam and Eve took the fruit representing Christ's conquering of sin. Paintings of the Immaculate Conception are allegories and difficult to understand. Mary will be the one to bear the child who will save man.

SALA 5: MANNERISM

There are three paintings from the "Mannerism" style, which refers to "later Renaissance."

- *Assumption with John the Baptist and Catherine of Alexandria* (Federico Zuccari, 1566). The style is "Roman Mannerist," a highly stylized and painting technique with the figures looking up in a melodramatic manner.

Mannerism Painting

Mannerism is confusing and subject to different interpretations but, in general usage, it describes art in Italy directly succeeding that of the Renaissance and before the Baroque Era. Initially it was a pejorative term to describe paintings that were melodramatic with dramatic distortion of bodies and lots of dark areas to create psychological tension. Michelangelo and Raphael were initial developers of this style.

- *Ecstasy of St. Margaret of Cortona* (Giuseppe Maria Crespi, 1701). This shows heavy use of chiaroscuro popularized by Titian and Caravaggio. The darkness of the scene is broken by flashes of light that reflect off the figures, particularly Christ and Margaret, creating a mystical link between the two. Margaret holds Christ's crown of thorns.
- *Miracle of San Francesco da Paola* (Francesco Capella, 1750). The painting shows a miracle of San Francesco da Paola, who with a gesture of his hand, saves a mason who has fallen from scaffolding. Two workers, busy with their work are unaware of the occurrence.

SALA 6: THE GREAT STAIRCASE

Sala 5. The Assumption by Federico Zuccari.

The great staircase by Filippo Berrettini was made more than a century after construction of the Church of Jesus in 1645. It connects the church with the oratory in the basement.

- At the bottom is a life-sized triumphant statue of *Christ the Redeemer*. The statue is placed in the Duomo during the Easter Season.
- The staircase is lined by modern cartoons depicting the *Way of the Cross* by Cortona artist Gino Severini, 1944. The pictures were ordered to fulfill a vow made by the Cortonese during WWII. The actual mosaics of the fourteen stations of the cross were installed on the path leading up to the Basilico of St. Margaret. Severini's designs were inspired by Cubism and Futurism.

SALA 7: THE ORATORY

Originally the room served as a point for meetings and ceremonies.

Christ Risen at the foot of the stairs to the Oratory.

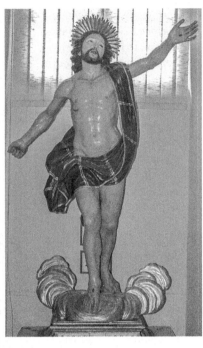

- The room is lined by a choir carved by Vicenzo di Pietropaolo, 1517.
- The ceiling is covered by frescoes from the workshop of Giorgio Vasari, executed by one of his students, Doceno, 1555. Vasari limited his participation to some sketching and touching up.
- At the end of the room is a polychrome terracotta of the *Pietà* with St. John, Mary, Mary of Bethany (see sidebar), Mary of Cleopas, and Mary Magdalen holding Christ's Body (Bernardino Covatti from the workshop of della Robbia, 1519).
- The fresco cycle on the walls, done by one of Vasari's students, shows sacrifices offered by characters of the Old Testament. It ends with the representation on the vault of three episodes from the New Testament, connecting the theme of transition from the Old to the New Testament. The twelve sacrificing figures are, starting from the entrance door:

The della Robbia Pietà in the Oratory.

- On the right wall: Nehemiah, Samuel, Aaron, Moses, Jacob. On the front wall: Cain (damaged), Abel (damaged).
- On the left wall from the back of the oratory: Isaac, Abraham, Enoch, Melchizedek, and Noah (damaged).
- On the vault: Transfiguration, Descent to Limbo, and Conversion of Saul.
- Further decorative elements represent the twelve virtues.
- The *Evangelists and Two Scenes from the New Testament* (Florentine school, Andrea del Minga, 1560). These include the Last Supper and Christ Praying in the Garden of Gethsemane.

> **The Marys at the Crucifixion**
>
> The Three Marys refers to a set of three women mentioned in the New Testament considered to have been pious followers of Christ. The name "Mary" was common in the old testament.
>
> Two of the Marys are obvious: Mary, Christ's mother, and Mary of Magdalen. Scholars don't agree on the third Mary and it may have been Mary of Bethany, Mary Salome the Disciple, Mary mother of James the Less, Mary of Cleopas, Mary of Rome, or Mary, mother of John Mark of Jerusalem. Another factor confusing the issue is that there may have been one set of Marys at the cross, another at the entombment, and still another at the empty tomb.

SALA 8: TREASURY HALL

The hall includes a rare collection of precious liturgical objects produced from local workshops. The most prestigious pieces come from Siena, Florence, and Rome. Note particularly:

- *Casali Chalice* (Michele di Tommè, 1370) gilded, embossed, and sculpted in silver and copper. It sits on a base of six cherubs heads and flowers. The center knot is formed by six hexagonal sides, one with the coat of arms of the Casali family. The base includes six characters, four are identified: John the Baptist, St. Benedict, St. Catherine of Alexandria, and St. Margaret of Cortona.
- *Vagnucci's Reliquary* (Giusto da Firenze, 1457). Fused and sculpted gold, silver, and copper; translucent and opaque enamels, rock crystal, vitreous pastes, semiprecious pearls and stones. Jacopo Vagnucci came into possession of a relic from the garment that Christ wore when he healed a woman suffering from continuous hemorrhage. The statue on the right is Pope Nicholas V and on the left is Pope Gregory III.
- *Colbert Chalice* (Vincenzo Brugo, 1845). Gold and silver. The cup is surrounded by a relief of the Last Supper. The base has sculpted reliefs of the Crucifixion, Deposition, and Resurrection. Under the foot of the chalice is a dedication: "My Lord Jesus Christ, on behalf of the daughters of my institutions of St. Anne and St. Mary Magdalen and for me, be

a sacrifice for the expiation of our sins, for the fulfillment of our merited pains, for gratitude for the grace which we have received and for the request of that grace which we will need."

Additional items in Sala 8:

- Stone matrix for a crucifix and seventh century earring from Farneta.
- A cross to be carried on a pole of the twelfth century.
- A chalice/ciborium of Aretine workmanship (14th c.) of gilded copper engraved with translucent and opaque enamels.
- Italian made ciborium (15th c.) of engraved gilded copper.
- A reliquary cross, Tuscan (16th c.) of gilded copper and silver.
- Three vases for holy oil in silver (16th c.).

SALA 9: PARATO PASSERINI — VESTMENTS

The Tapestry, made around 1517 was commissioned by Cardinal Silvio Passerini to be worn by Pope Leo X de' Medici during his visit in Cortona. It is made up of a chasuble, a dalmatica, a tunicle, a cope, two stoles, three fanons, an altar frontal, a lectern cover and a chalice bag. The embroideries of the altar frontal and of the cope hood have been created on the basis of some drawings by Andrea del Sarto, while those of the chasuble and of the altar frontal stole are inspired by drawings of Raffaellino del Garbo.

10 Duomo della Santa Maria Assunta

Location:

43.276411, 11.98398

Piazza del Duomo, 1
A short distance from Piazza Signorelli.

Hours:

Daily Summer: 07.30-13.00, 15.30-18.30
Daily Winter: 08.00-12.30, 15.00-17.30

Also varies on holidays and times of services.

Time to visit: About an hour.

Reasons for a visit: Though not as ornate as Pisa or Siena, it has several good pieces of art and a statue of George Washington — at least it looks like him. The piazza in front of the church provides expansive views of the Valdichiana, especially when the valley is covered by fog and Cortona sits above it.

Photography: Yes.

Accessibility: Once you get up the couple of steps in the front it is clear going.

Below: the George Washington look-alike statue in the Duomo.

Highlights

Built on the ruins of a pagan temple and documented as a church in the eleventh century, the present church was begun in 1480 and finished in 1507 in a mixture of Renaissance and Baroque styles. It was elevated to the status of "cathedral" in 1507, the bishop's church (the names *cattedrale* or duomo indicate the presence of a bishop in the city). The bell tower was added in 1556.

Exterior

The façade has traces of buildings from different eras. The oldest remnants date back to a medieval Romanesque façade with a pillar

The ceiling is one of the most interesting features of the Duomo, but take some binoculars. St. Leo I is in the more central circle.

and columns at the corners. Medieval elements include the long narrow window and a marble slab with a fourteenth century coat of arms.

There are two entrances to the church. The elegant main entrance at the front has two sandstone columns with bas-relief images of St. Michael the Archangel on the right and the Lion of St. Mark on the left. The porch provides a color contrast to the walls with delicate moldings shaping the base.

The second entrance is on the side of the church and features a sandstone gate with bas-relief figures of flowers, animals and other symbols.

Interior

The church has a nave and two side aisles divided by columns. Many of the works of art came from other Cortona churches but the best works have been moved to the Museo Diocesano directly across the piazza from the Duomo.

- On the interior façade wall is a balcony for the choir and organ and above that is a rose window, not stained glass, but remarkably detailed.
- Immediately on the right side of the entrance is a statue of a dignitary who bears a striking resemblance, in both features and pose, to George Washington.
- The arched Gothic ceiling over the aisles and nave is gracefully designed with vaults supported by gently curved and pointed Gothic arches. The ceiling is covered with a bright blue background and gold stars, much like the basilica in Assisi and the Basilica di Santa Margherita at the top of the hill.

Reliquary with over 100 relics in the first right side altar.

RIGHT AISLE SIDE ALTARS

- First right side altar: The Chapel of the Reliquary. Behind glass is a valuable collection of more than 100 relics donated by Basilio Brunori (1879).
- Second right side altar: the Chapel of the *Transfiguration of Christ* (Raffaello Vanni, 17th c.). It's a Mannerist style painting with a lot melodrama portrayed by the figures around Christ.
- Third right side altar: the Chapel of the Virgin with a painting of the *Madonna with the Baby Jesus and John the Baptist* (16th c.).
- Fourth right side altar: The *Death of St. Joseph* (Lorenzo Berrettini, 17th c.).

PULPIT

- The *Pulpit* is elaborately and finely carved wood with a spiral staircase (Michelangiolo Leggi, 1524).

The Transfiguration by Raffaello Vanni.

Madonna del Pianto, 13th c., right front altar.

RIGHT FRONT ALTAR

- The right side altar next to the high altar is the Chapel of the Madonna del Pianto with an important terracotta sculpture (13th c.) of the *Madonna del Pianto* (Our Lady of Tears), which at first glance appears crudely carved. However, when you get closer, Mary's face shows an intense sorrow and devastation at the death of her son. Christ's blood runs down His side over His covering.
- On the right wall is the entrance to the sacristy, closed to visitors.
- The organ was built in 1517 and restored in 1720.

HIGH ALTAR

- The carved marble high altar is a masterpiece of Baroque style. The tabernacle rests high above the altar with ornate sets of candles held by angels guarding each side (Francesco Mazzuoli, 1664).
- At the very top is a portrait of *Our Lady of the Germans*.
- Hanging above the altar is a *baldacchino*, a canopy that resembles a crown.

CHOIR AND APSE

Unfortunately, since the first edition of this book, the apse is often closed to visitors. There are several interesting works, including the ceiling. If the caretaker is around, ask to cross the barrier into the apse.

- Behind the altar is the choir with two rows of seats and a modern electronic organ. The choir seats were made by Vinchenzo Conti and Stefano Fabbrucci (late 17th c.).
- The frescoes in the choir ceiling (Brunacci) vaults depict images of *Faith, Hope, Charity, and Peace*.

High altar in the Duomo.

- In the upper portion of the back window is a stained glass (Giuseppe Ciotti, 1960) depicting *Blessed Pietro Cappucci and Venerable Veronica Lapareli*.

- On the back of the altar are the *Crucifixion* (school of Signorelli), the *Incredulity of St. Thomas* (school of Luca Signorelli), the *Assumption with Saints* (Giuseppe Ciotti), and *Madonna of the Sacred Belt* (Cristoforo Allori).

- On the right wall are the *Madonna of the Rosary* (Cigoli, 1567), *Consecration of the Basilica del Salvatore* (Andrea Commodi, 1603), and the *Descent of the Holy Spirit* (Tommaso Bernabei).

- On the left wall are the *Virgin with Baby and St. Gaetano* (Giovanni Maria Morandi), the *Guardian Angel* (Giovanni Grati, 1781), and the *Assumption* (Andrea del Sarto).

LEFT FRONT ALTAR

- The Chapel of the Blessed Sacrament with the *Communion of Our Lady* (Salvi Castellucci, 17th c.) with rich, brilliant colors. Someone holds the Eucharistic host preparing to give it to Mary.

Intricately carved pulpit in the Duomo.

Mosaic of Christ the Redeemer (Gino Severini, 20th c.)

- On the altar in the left aisle is the painting of the *Adoration of the Shepherds* by Pietro da Cortona (1663).
- To the immediate right of the altar is a small, modern mosaic with a rainbow of colors of *Christ the Redeemer* by contemporary Cortona artist Gino Severini (20th c.).
- Next to the mosaic is *Ciborium in Marble* (Urbano da Cortona, 1491) with a small wooden door surrounded by an ornate marble frame with columns and lunette.

LEFT SIDE ALTARS

- First left side altar: the Chapel of the Blessed Guido with a painting of the *Madonna with Saints Philip Neri, Margherita da Cortona, Blessed Guido, and Ugolino* (Lorenzo Berrettini, 17th c.). Beneath the altar is the ossuary of the Blessed Guido Vagnottelli, a Franciscan Friar.
- Second left side altar: the Chapel of the Crucifixion has a large *Crucifixion* in wood (Andrea Sellari, 17th c.). The crucifix doesn't quite show the strain in the muscles as He slumps forward in death. The crown of thorns is long and vicious.
- Third left side altar: the Chapel of the Nativity with a painting of the *Nativity of Christ* (Pietro Berrettini, 17th c.).
- Fourth left side altar: *San Sebastiano* (Lazzaro Baldi, 17th c.).
- Fifth side altar: the Chapel of the Madonna degli Alemanni (Our Lady of the Germans). The terracotta of the *Our Lady of the Germans* (15th c.) is believed to be miraculous.

10 Duomo della Santa Maria Assunta

The miraculous terracotta of the Madonna degli Alemanni.

Chocolate Mousse

Ah, yes, Italians do like chocolate — a lot. When my cousin serves this delectable, light mousse for the *dolce* there are no leftovers.

Ingredients

1-3/4 c chilled heavy whipping cream, divided
12 oz semi-sweet chocolate chips
3 oz espresso or strong coffee
4 T butter
1 t flavorless gelatin

Directions

- Chill 1-1/2 c of whipping cream and put the mixing bowl and whisk or beaters in the freezer.
- In the top of a double boiler combine chocolate chips, 1/4 c cream, coffee, and butter. Melt over low simmering water stirring constantly. Remove from the heat when it has all melted.
- Cool to about 100 degrees. Put the remainder of the cream (1/4 c) in a small pan and sprinkle the gelatin over it. Carefully heat over very low heat, stirring constantly. Do not boil! Then stir the mixture into the cooled chocolate and set aside so it sets.
- Take the equipment and rest of the cream from the refrigerator. Whip the cream and fold into the chocolate mixture. Do not over stir, it's OK to have some streaks.
- Chill for at least an hour and then serve.

11 Chiesa di San Domenico

Location:

43.273964, 11.989152

Largo Beato Angelico, 1
Outside the Via Nazionale gate.

Website (Italian): http://www.cortona.ws/chiesa_domenico_it.html

Hours: 09.00 to 17.00

Time to visit: Twenty minutes.

Reasons for a visit: The restored magnificent altarpiece. There are few better. There are several excellent paintings including one of St. Catherine of Alexandria.

Photography: Yes.

Accessibility: Several steps to get up to the entrance door. An additional five steps up to the presbytery — the altar and apse area.

BACKGROUND

Early documents put a hospice on this site in 1230. It was replaced by a convent and small church in 1440. During a period of peace after Florence extended its control throughout most of Tuscany the Dominican order constructed a larger church. Further restorations were completed in 1594.

EXTERIOR

- The plain stone façade is typical of the Dominican and other mendicant orders like the Franciscans.
- In the lunette above the door is a partially restored fresco by Fra Angelico of the *Madonna with Saints Dominic and Peter the Martyr* (1433-1434).

INTERIOR

If the interior is too dim, there is a box as you enter. Put a euro in it and you'll have light for about ten minutes.

The Virgin with Souls in Purgatory, third right side altar.

- The interior is a single nave with five steps up to the presbytery.
- At one time the walls were frescoed, but today only fragments remain. The best of those remaining were moved to the Museo Diocesano.
- Immediately to the right is a painting of the *Pietà* (Baccio Ponetti, 17th c.).
- On the front wall near the entrance are two fresco fragments: *Sant'Agostino* (Marcillat) and *San Rocco* (Bartolomeo della Gatta, 15th c.).

Right Side Altars

- First right side altar: A life-sized statue of the *Crucifixion* (14th c.) behind glass on red background.
- Next is a fresco fragment of events in the life of *Santa Caterina di Siena* (Bartolomeo della Gatta, 15th c.).
- Second right side altar: Statue of the *Crowned Mary* (Francesco Fabbrucci, 18th c.), her face showing unmitigated sorrow. Three daggers on one side and four on the other piercing her breast represent the "Seven Sorrows of Mary."
- Third right side altar: The *Virgin with Souls of Purgatory* (Pietro con Batti, 1775). A larger figure, a Dominican nun (on the left) pours water on people in purgatory who are sitting within flames of purification.

Right Front Altar

- Portrait of *San Domenico* with one of his symbols, lilies.
- *Virgin and Franciscan Saints* (Luca Signorelli).
- *Deposition* (Baccio Bonetti).

HIGH ALTAR: ALTARPIECE — POLYPTYCH

The most important work in the church is the magnificent polyptych altarpiece by Lorenzo di Nicolò (1402). It was donated to the church by Cosimo Medici in 1420. It has eight panels with a five part predella along the bottom. The altarpiece has been restored to pristine condition with pure, bright colors and expressive details. Even the columns along the sides have six scenes painted on them.

[**Note:** There are two lights on either side of the altar that can be plugged in. It takes several minutes for the lights to warm up.]

The center panel shows *Christ Crowning Mary* in heaven with six angels playing music below and ten saints on the side panels.

Details from the altarpiece. Top: Christ crowning Mary with the apostles on both sides.

- The upper panels show *Christ Crucified* and *Christ Resurrected* in the center and the *Annunciation* on the two sides with St. Gabriel on the left and Mary on the right.
- On the side pillars are twenty unidentified saints.
- The left and right panels show a number of saints. The center character on the right is San Domenico. The three characters on the right are John the Baptist, St. John the Evangelist, and St. Paul, with the sword. The martyred saints hold small palm leaves that look like feathers.
- The center image on the predella shows the three magi worshiping Christ. The other panels depict events from the life of a saint.
- Beneath the simple, limestone altar is the body of a Dominican, Beato Pietro Capucci da Tiferno (d. 1445). In 1516 Pope Leo X gave permission to the Cortonese to display the body.

LEFT FRONT ALTAR

- *Mary Holding the Baby with San Domenico and Bishop*. Mary's feet rest on the heads of two cherubs and two angels stand behind Mary. The bishop shows evidence of the stigmata (Luca Signorelli, 16th c.).

The two side panels represent the Annunciation. Gabriel, left, carries God's request to Mary, right, to become the mother of the Son of God.

LEFT SIDE ALTARS

- First side altar: *Assumption of the Virgin with St. Hyacinth and Dominican Saints* (Jacopo Negretti, early 17th c.). On the lower half the confused apostles are looking heavenward, while Mary is guided by angels, some playing lutes.
- Second side altar: The *Circumcision of Christ* (Domenico Cresti, 1598). Mary stands on the left in her red dress and blue robe. Jesus is held over a bowl to collect the blood. The painting is rich in detailed story-telling details with elaborate robes and embroidered cloth, typical of the Vasari's Mannerism style.
- Third side altar: Palei coat of arms. The *Dispute of Santa Caterina d'Alessandria* (Andrea Commodi, 1603). Santa Caterina is attempting to convert the Emperor to Christianity, instead she is sentenced to death on the wheel. When she touches the wheel it breaks and then she is beheaded. (The broken wheel is usually in paintings of St. Catherine from Alexandria.)

Santa Caterina d'Alessandria is put on trial before the Sultan. Note the broken wheel at her feet.

12 Chiesa di San Francesco

Location:

43.275465, 11.986785
Piazza San Francesco
Via Berretinni and Via Maffei

Website (Italian): http://www.cortona.ws/chiesa_francesco_it.html

Hours: Daily: 09.00-19.00

Time to visit: Thirty minutes to view art works and relics.

Reasons for a visit: There are probably hundreds of churches dedicated to San Francesco, however this is special. Inside are important relics of the saint and a relic of the True Cross.

Photography: No. Video surveillance.

Accessibility: A bunch of steep steps to get up to the entrance door. A relic of the True Cross is kept above the altar but you have to climb a set of very narrow steps, less than two-feet wide, to view the reliquary of the True Cross.

The steps up to the church are steep, rough, and many.

Background

Built in 1245 upon former Etruscan and Roman baths, the church uses the typical Gothic-Franciscan style: a broad nave ending with an apse vault flanked by two smaller chapels. Friar Elia Coppi created the designs for the church. Except for the façade, most of the original Gothic elements were lost during a seventeenth century restoration. The ceiling is typical Franciscan with simple wooden trusses. The reconstruction did a lot of damage; it plastered over the fourteenth century frescoes and replaced them with altars. The Gothic windows on the right side were replaced with rectangular windows, the left side windows were bricked in, and the crypt was filled with debris.

Exterior

- The façade is the soaring Gothic style with typical Franciscan simplicity: plain, rough sandstone with a marble archivolt.
- The lancet arched main door (16th c.) has three narrow columns along the side.

Detail of St. Francis discussing faith with the Sultan.

- A small crucifix stands at the peak of the roof.
- The *Crowning of the Virgin* is in the lunette.
- Originally there was a large, rose window; however it was closed off and a plain, ugly, square window installed.

INTERIOR

- The interior has a single wide nave. Another fine example of simple Franciscan design is the Basilica di San Francesco in nearby Arezzo. The Franciscans took a vow of poverty and did not use money for elegant and expensive decorations.
- In the church there are busts of the twelve apostles in small Gothic niches.
- On the left wall are fragments of an *Annunciation* (Jacopo di Mino del Pellicciaio, 14th c.).
- The raised, ancient pews have ornate carved backs. When sitting against them you are definitely doing penance.
- To the left of the entrance is a painting of *Friar Elias* and a fresco fragment of the *Crowned Virgin in Glory among Saints* (Diro Ferri).

RIGHT SIDE ALTARS

- First right side altar: the Capulli Altar dedicated to St. Francis and St. Bonaventure. A vivid painting of *San Francesco in Front of the Sultan* (Nicolò Monti di Pistoia, 1842).

- Immediately to the left of the first side altar is a statue of the *Risen Christ*.
- Second right side altar: Rotani Altar dedicated to St. Anne: The *Meeting of San Joachim and St. Anne at the Gate of Aurea*. (Orazio Fidani, 1645). Very dark.
- Third right side altar: Sernini Cucciatti Altar. An allegory of the *Immaculate Conception with Santi Cristoforo, Ludovico, Giuseppe Cillia, Caterina* (Andrea Commodi, 1609). Immaculate Conception paintings are allegories. Mary is usually at the top and there are several baby heads or cherubs in the picture. San Ludovico Re (the king) is painted in the center bottom. The theme is a reference to the change coming to the world.
- Between the third and fourth altars is a statue of *Sant'Antonio di Padova* with the Child Jesus.
- Fourth right side altar: Tommasi Altar. Painting of *Sant'Antonio di Padova and the Miracle of the Mule* (Ludovico Cardi, aka Il Cigoli, 1597).
- Fifth right side altar: Baldelli Altar dedicated to San Francesco and Santa Margherita da Cortona. *Madonna and Child in Glory with Saints Francesco, Margherita da Cortona, and Niccolò* (Rustici, 1625).

Top: The high altar with relic of the True Cross.

Above: The ivory tablet holding a small relic of the True Cross, the cross of Christ's crucifixion.

One of the habits worn by San Francesco.

FRONT RIGHT SIDE ALTAR

- On the right is a fresco of the *Madonna con Bambino* above the altar (14th c.).
- On the right wall is the monument to one of the bishops of Cortona (1348).

HIGH ALTAR AND RELIC OF THE TRUE CROSS

- The marble high altar is Baroque.
- A narrow, hidden set of about 10 steps enables you to climb to the height of the tabernacle to see the relic of the True Cross.
- The magnificent marble tabernacle and reliquary rises above the altar (Bernardino Radi, 1619) holding a piece of the True Cross given Friar Elia Coppi by the Greek Emperor of Nicea, Giovanni III in 1244. The reliquary is engraved with 31 biblical scenes and 15 silver statuettes. On the front of the ivory tablet is a gold filigree cross which houses a fragment of the Cross. On the back (not visible) are two inscriptions in Greek
- Friar Elia, a close friend of San Francesco, served as an envoy for Federico II in Constantinople and was presented with the relic there. Elia's tomb, in the choir, is memorialized by a simple slab.
- The tabernacle is a large, square shape that sits on small legs representing the apostles. At the first tier in the Tabernacle (Cesarino da Perugia, 1518) is a statue of St. Peter on the left and St. John the Evangelist on the right.

THE CHOIR

- The U-shaped choir is behind the altar. It is a small room about twelve-feet square with seats separated by arm rests around three sides of the room.
- On the left wall is a painting of a *Pope Praying to Christ* with a book and skull.
- On the right wall is the *Assumption*.
- Atop the wall that backs to the altar is a portrait of Friar Elia.
- In the center of the floor is the tombstone of Fra Elia Coppi.

LEFT FRONT SIDE ALTAR

- Here is a statue of San Francesco, unusual because he wears a black robe, rather than the plain brown habit in which he is usually depicted.
- Below the statue and altar is a glass case holding important relics of San Francesco. Carbon dating completed in 2007 indicate that these relics definitely came from the time of St. Francis:
  - a habit,
  - an embroidered funeral pillow from Jacopa di Settisole on which the dying San Francesco laid his head, and
  - his new testament given to him by Friar Elia.

The Coronation of the Virgin by Jacopo di Mino del Pellicciaio, third left side altar.

LEFT SIDE ALTARS

- First left side altar: Baldacchini altar dedicated to the Crucifix. Today's wooden *Crucifix* (Fabbrucci, 17th c.) replaces the thirteenth century original, now in the Basilica di Santa Margherita. St. Margaret said her prayers before the crucifix now in the Basilica. The background painting depicts *Santa Margherita and San Giuseppe di Copertino*.
- Second left side altar: dedicated to the *Annunciation* (Pietro Berrettini da Cortona, 1669).
- Between the second and third side altar is a large painting of the *Martyrdom of Santa Lucia* (Giovan Camillio Sagrestani, 1730).
- Third left side altar: Zefferini altar dedicated to Saints Jerome and Lucy. The fresco is the *Coronation of the Virgin with a Young Saint* (Jacopo di Mino del Pellicciaio, 14th c.) with a fragment of the Annunciation. Angels are playing music and accompanying Mary, similar to the altarpiece in La Chiesa di San Domenico.
- Fourth left side altar: Tozzi altar dedicated to St. Joseph. The *Nativity* (Raffaello Vanni, 17th c.).

Veal Cutlets Braised in a Simple Tomato Sauce

This is a simpler but tasty recipe for veal from my cousin Marisa. Extensive browning is avoided to make sure that the veal is tender.

Ingredients

1-1/2 c of basic tomato sauce (see "Inside Tuscany: Arezzo")
four veal cutlets pounded thin (about 1/4-inch)
3 T drained and minced capers
handful of minced parsley
1 anchovy fillet minced
1/2 c flour

Directions

- Pour the sauce into a sauce pan large enough to hold the veal cutlets. Heat to a simmer.
- Trim any fat or gristle from the veal.
- Dredge the cutlets through the flour and place them in the pan with the sauce.
- Mince the capers, parsley, and anchovy together.
- Sprinkle the minced mixture over the cutlets.
- Turn them over and let cook for a couple of minutes on the other side.
- Serve.

13 Santuario di Santa Margherita

AKA the Basilica di Santa Margherita

Location:

43.276455, 11.99235
Via Santa Margherita 1

0575.603116
351.8027962

Email: santuariosantamargherita@gmail.com

Italian Site: https://santamargher-itadacortona.com/tempi-forti/

Facebook: Ospitalità a Santa Bargherita da Cortona:
https://www.facebook.com/Ospitalità-a-Santa-Margherita-da-Cortona-1468001276814233/

You can drive to the church, it has a large parking lot or take one of the trails. In fact, if you don't mind walking up the steep hill after touring the town, it is a good place to park for access to the town.

The first of two trails leading up the hill to the Santuario di Santa Margherita.

Hours:

Daily: 07.00-19.30

Time to visit: One hour.

Reasons for a visit: It is one of the most important basilicas in Tuscany with major art works and the "incorrupt" body of St. Margaret above the high altar. In late afternoon, the sunset is spectacular.

Fun: I enjoy walking up and down the steep trails even more than visiting the church.

Photography: Yes, though refrain from taking a picture of her body, especially if there are other people in line to view the relic.

Accessibility: If you drive to the piazza parking lot there are only a few steps up

The second trail begins at the end of Via Nazionale. It is lined with Severini's mosaics of the Stations of the Cross. This trail is not as steep as the other.

to the entrance. There are several narrow steps up to view Santa Margherita in her glass coffin above the high altar.

WALKING TO THE BASILICA — TWO TRAILS

TRAIL I

43.276278, 11.989844

The first time I looked for a path to the Santuario I started walking up the steep streets. I knew that the church stood at the top of the hill and figured that as long as I was walking up I'd find it, and I did. There was a nondescript yellow sign on the side of a building with an arrow marking the way to "S. Margherita." The wide trail is paved with rough stones and, though steep, anyone should be able to manage it by taking a slow pace and stopping to admire the view.

The yellow sign points the way to the basilica along Trail 1.

TRAIL 2: VIA DEL CROCIFISSO — WAY OF THE CROSS — VIA SANTA MARGHERITA

43.274963, 11.988952

Once at the top you'll notice that there is another trail. This is the one that is lined with Severini's mosaics of the fourteen Stations of the Cross. The ceramics were commissioned to honor Santa Margherita for sparing Cortona from bombings during WWII. An additional mosaic on the path shows *Santa Margherita Praying before the Crucifix*. The stations start where the trail begins in a lower portion of Cortona at Via Santa Margherita. This trail is more gradual, though you'll still know that it is uphill.

HIGHLIGHTS

The church is dedicated to Santa Margherita, patron saint of Cortona. The building was completed in 1304, but continued to be embellished with important frescoes (Lorenzetti brothers' workshop) throughout the fourteenth century. Only a few fragments survive in the Diocesan Museum.

Santa Margherita

Santa Margherita was born in 1247 into a farming family at Laviano, a small village in the area of Perugia. Her mother died when she was eight, her father remarried and her childhood and adolescence were burdened by abuse from her stepmother, jealous of Margaret's beauty.

Margaret's beauty attracted the attention of Arsenio, a wealthy nobleman of Montepulciano. Though she was only sixteen, Arsenio promised her marriage and she became the man's mistress. She bore him a son, but he never married her. During their nine years together Margaret enjoyed a wealthy life with clothing and jewels. After nine years Arsenio was killed under mysterious circumstances and she was expelled from his castle alone and penniless with a small son.

Severini's mosaic of the Ninth Station of the Cross on the second path to the church.

She survived as a prostitute and later lived with another aristocrat. Despite her immoral life God never abandoned her. God spoke through her heart and she left the man and put herself under the guidance of the Franciscans; she was 25. After three years of penance and charitable works she was admitted to the Franciscan Third Order of Penance and then founded the Hospital of St. Mary of Mercy in Cortona.

Margaret prayed to a crucifix that was originally in the Chiesa di San Francesco. Christ would come down from the cross to talk with her. After sixteen years, it was difficult to hide her mystical experiences with Christ from others. At the command of Christ she went further up the hill, just under the fort, and into a solitary cell attached to the Church of St. Basil and lived as a recluse for nine years. For the last seventeen days of her life, Margaret neither ate nor drank. Just before sunrise on 27 February 1297 her face radiated joy and beauty and she died. Those present sensed a mysterious sweetness and could smell a fragrance recognized as

Detail from the Ecstasy of Santa Caterina d'Alessandria at the first right side altar.

a sign of grace and holiness. She was canonized in Rome on 16 May 1728.

INTERIOR

- Immediately on the right of the entrance door is a painting of *Margherita Receiving the Franciscan Habit of the Third Order* (Sante Pacini, 1775).
- The vaulted ceiling is painted blue with gold stars and red triangles, much like the basilica in Assisi (Giuseppe Bandini and Gaetano Grunacci, 1880-1881).
- The dome has a round window decorated with red, blue, and yellow patterns.
- The rose window on the front wall is composed of plain pieces of glass in an elaborate pattern. In front of it is a large choir balcony with a huge organ.
- On four of the columns in the nave are four glazed terracotta statues of saints by Amalia Duprè di Siena (1886-1889). Left nearest the entrance: San Luigi, King of France. Left toward the altar: San Francesco. Right nearest entrance: Santa Elisabetta, Queen of Hungary. Right toward altar: Santa Chiara.
- To the left of the entrance door is a painting of *Santa Margherita holding a Child at a Baptism* (Filippo Burci, 1775).

RIGHT SIDE

- First right side altar: above the Baldelli altar is a much worn painting of the *Ecstasy of Santa Caterina d'Alessandria* (Barocci di Urbino, 1610). The colors are still clear and bright but the canvas is cracked and flaking.
- After the first side altar is a memorial to *Pope John Paul II*.

- Second right side altar: above the Laparelli altar is a picture of the *Assumption with John the Baptist* with saints Diego di Alcala and Chiara (Jacopo Chimenti da Empoli, 1606). The altar is dedicated to Fra Bartolomeo Tommasi and Fra Gian Gastone Laparelli, commandants in the navy and members of the Order of the Knights of Malta, 1736. The flags and lanterns come from Turkish Muslim warships sunk in the Mediterranean.

> **Incorrupt Remains**
>
> An incorrupt body is spared decomposition. Mummification, as in the case of Santa Margherita, is not an indication of decomposition. (Seems like splitting hairs to me.)

- After the right second side altar is a beautiful statue of the *Mourning Madonna*.

Right Front Altar

- On the right wall is a reliquary banner.
- To the left of the banner is a marble sculpture of *Santa Margherita*.
- Above the Altar of the Crucifixion is a dramatic wood sculpture of the *Crucifixion* on a red silk background (13th c.). The arms and torso are impossibly long, but the lack of realism does not get in the way of the emotional impact. Originally the crucifix was housed in the Church of San Francesco. According to Santa Margherita's confessor Christ came down from the cross, opened the doors to the church, and had long conversations with her.

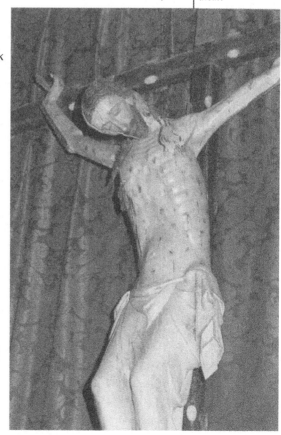

Crucifixion above the right front altar.

High Altar and Tomb of Santa Margherita

- The altar is decorated in a Rococo style with much scroll work and different colored marble. The crucifix above is flanked by six-foot tall candles.
- Upon the main altar is a silver and glass coffin

High Altar with the incorrupt body of Santa Margherita.

holding the "incorrupt" mummified body of Santa Margherita (Pietro Berrettini, 1646). She was quite short, perhaps only four-feet tall.

- The casket rests within an urn bordered by a frame of embossed and engraved silver.

CHOIR BEHIND THE HIGH ALTAR

- Behind the altar is the carved wooden choir with a small organ.
- The right wall has a painting of the *Ecstasy of Santa Margherita* (Giuseppe Fabbrini, 1771).
- The left wall has a painting of the *Apparition of the Baby Jesus to Santa Margherita* (Gesualdo Ferri, 1775).

Left Front Altar

- The Altar of the Blessed Sacrament.
- Statue of *San Francesco*.
- On the left side of the altar is a marble sarcophagus originally intended to hold the body of Santa Margherita (Angelo and Francesco di Pietro, 1362). The predella recounts events from her life: receiving the habit, putting the habit on, helping others, and being laid in the tomb.

Left Side

- The first stop after the left front altar is a chapel dedicated to the fallen soldiers of World War I. Frescoes were done by Osvaldo Bignami, 1917.
- After the chapel is a statue dedicated to *Sant'Antonio di Padova*. He is holding the child Christ upon a bible with his tongue (taken out when martyred) in his right hand. Above the altar are ghosts of soldiers with Santa Margherita in front and Jesus to the side. My family, Tiezzi, is listed.
- The first left side altar (after the war memorial chapel): above the Alticozzi altar is a picture of the *Slaughter of the Innocents* (Giannotti Pietro da Bolognese, 1636).
- Last side altar on the left: the Lucci altar. A picture of the *Immaculate Conception with Santi Francesco, Domenico, Ludovico, and Blessed Margherita* (Francesco Vanni, 1602). Blessed Margherita was later canonized in 1728. Paintings of the Immaculate Conception are difficult to interpret and this is more mysterious than most.
- *God Our Merciful Father* painting.

Detail from the Slaughter of the Innocents on the first left side altar.

Marisa's Lemon Cake — Torta Limone

Marisa was my cousin. She was a fireball of energy and a master cook who made her meals based on what was fresh in her husband Nando's two-acre garden. She taught us this on a visit with us in 2000. This recipe also works well at high altitude.

<u>Ingredients</u>

2 eggs
1 c plain yogurt
1 c oil
1 c sugar
1-1/2 c flour
1 t baking powder
zest of one lemon

<u>Directions</u>

- Preheat oven to 350°.
- Combine dry ingredients.
- Thoroughly mix in eggs, yogurt, oil, and lemon zest.
- Pour into small, greased cake pan. Recipe can be doubled for a full-sized cake pan.
- Bake about 40 minutes, until a toothpick inserted in the center comes out clean.
- Dust with powdered sugar before serving or drizzle a little limoncello over it.

14 Chiesa di San Niccolò

Location:

43.27565, 11.99014

Piazza San Niccolò 1
0575.604591

Email: c

Website (Italian):
http://www.cortona.ws/chiesa_niccolo_it.html

Facebook: https://www.facebook.com/pages/Chiesa-di-San-Niccolò-Cortona/267482256740161

You have to climb almost all the way up the Cortona hill. You will be only a few yards from finding the trail to the Santuario di Santa Margherita.

Hours:

The hours vary and are different every year I visit. Perhaps the following will work:

Daily: 11.00-13.00, 15.00-18.00

Basically, the hours depend on the caretaker: whether he is there or not and whether he is in the mood to open the door.

Donation of at least €3.00 required.

Time to visit: Ten to twenty minutes.

Reasons for a visit: A prized double-sided exceptional Luca Signorelli altarpiece.

Photography: Absolutely not! They'll beat the crap out of you — not really, but almost.

Signorelli's Deposition in San Niccolò on the front side of the double panel painting. (WGA)

Fresco on the wall of the Madonna and Child between Saints. (WGA)

Accessibility: Several steps to get up to the door.

The Church

Leading to the small church is a private gravel courtyard lined with cypress and surrounded by walls. The trees shade the courtyard, it is a pleasant place to stop and relax, especially in the oppressive summer heat. It makes you forget the hustle and bustle of lower Cortona. A simple roof supported by four columns covers the front of the church and shelters the entrance.

Built in 1510 it was remodeled in the seventeenth and eighteenth centuries. The latest restorations were made in the 1950's.

Inside it has a finely carved wood coffered ceiling. There are two side altars.

There is a panel on the altar with paintings on both sides. On the front is the *Deposition of Christ* (Signorelli, 1510). Christ is surrounded by several saints including, on the left Dominic and Francis and on the right, Michael the Archangel, Mary Magdalen, and John the Baptist.

On the back of this painting is the *Madonna and Child between Saints Peter and Paul* (Signorelli, c. 1510).

On the left wall is a mostly complete fresco from the workshop of Signorelli of the *Madonna between Saints.* On the back left are Saints Rocco and Sebastian. Lower left Saints Christopher and Paul. The only one I know on the right is the hermit San Girolamo.

Beside the door is a book where Gino Severini painted a watercolor of San Niccolò.

15 Chiesa di San Cristoforo

43.276323, 11.989478

Piazza San Cristoforo

Intersection of Via San Niccolò and Via dell'Orto della Cera

This small church is only about 50-feet from San Niccolò near the top of the Cortona hill. The first trail to the Basilica di Santa Margherita is nearby.

Website: http://www.en.cortonaguide.com/san_cristoforo.html

Hours:

Every Saturday: 11.00-13.00, 15.00-18.00

These hours vary. Sometimes the doors are left open during off hours.

Reason to visit: There are several good frescoes from the Umbrian-Senese school inside the church and in the small chapel outside.

The small interior of San Cristoforo.

Fresco of the Crucifixion, Annunciation, and Ascension.

Accessibility: Fair. There is only one step to negotiate to enter, but it is crowded inside.

Background

According to a plaque in the left hand wall the Romanesque church was consecrated in 1192, which makes it one of the oldest in Cortona. The inscription on the plaque probably dates from 1705, when restoration of an ancient altar unearthed documents from the twelfth century.

Interior

- On the left wall is a thirteenth century fresco of the *Crucifixion*. The left panel depicts the Annunciation and the right shows the Ascension. In the lunette is teh risen Christ.
- An organ built in 1856 by Giovanni Bianci was renovated in 1978 and is Bianci's only surviving work.
- Above the main altar is a painting of *The Madonna and Child* with saints Christopher and Jerome.
- In the choir loft are two paintings: *Christ Cures a Man* and *Madonna and Child* between Michael the Archangel and another saint.
- Below the choir loft is a faded fresco of the *Madonna and Child with a Saint*.
- On the right wall is a fresco of the *Madonna and Child with Saints Catherine from Alexandria and John*.

EXTERIOR CHAPEL OF THE NATIVITY

Outside the church is a niche — or small chapel — with a fresco of the *Madonna and Child* with the *Annunciation* over the altar. Mary looks shocked when the angel appears to give her God's request to bear His son.

The church has a splendid double bell tower that sits dramatically against a clear blue sky (use a polarizer to accent the effect when taking a picture).

Above: Madonna and Child with Saints Christopher and Jerome.

Below: Detail from the Annunciation in the small exterior chapel.

The Chapel of the Nativity, a small niche outside the main church of San Cristoforo, is usually open. It has a fresco of the Annunciation and another of the Enthroned Madonna and Child.

16 Other Churches in Cortona

CHIESA DI SAN MARCO

43.274963, 11.988951: Lower Entrance.

Vicolo San Marco 1

Website: http://www.en.cortonaguide.com/san_marco.html

Hours:

Every Sunday 11.00-13.00, 15.00-18.00

The chief item of interest is the mosaic (by Gino Severini, 1951) above the lower entrance of St. Mark holding a bible with a lion (his symbol) at his feet.

The church was built on the site of an old pilgrim's hospital in the 1580s. There are two chapels, one over the other joined by a staircase. I've read that the lower church has frescoed vaults and a number of paintings, though I've never seen it. It is always closed to me. It is enough to see the grand mosaic.

CHIESA DI SANT'ANTONIO ABATE

43.266801, 11.958109

Website: http://www.en.cortonaguide.com/antonio_abate.html

Located near the Bacchus water tank of the Roman era are the remains of the Church of St. Anthony Abbot.

This church is closed. Outside the front façade in a niche built into a stone wall is an eroded statue of Sant'Antonio Abate. The church dates from 1300.

Chiesa della Santa Maria Nuova

43.278799, 11.989157

Via Santa Maria Nuova 116
Outside the walls.

333.7216112

Facebook: https://www.facebook.com/pages/Santa-Maria-Nuova-Cortona/284631358400872

Santa Maria Nuova

This is one of those churches that I never seem to find open but seems to be worth the effort. I was close to getting in last time; the outer doors were open but the inner glass doors were locked while people inside were preparing it for a wedding. It looked beautiful, something worth entering. It has a large parking lot, yet it is still close to the walls of Cortona, so if you can't find parking anywhere else, you could use the church's.

The following is information that I picked up from other sources:

The Church, in the shape of a Greek cross, was built, in part, in 1543 to 1550 by Giorgio Vasari (hometown, Arezzo).

Works of art:

- *Nativity* (Alessandro Allori, aka Bronzino).
- Stained glass: *San Carlo Borromeo Carries the Eucharist to Plague Victims* (pupil of Marcillat, see windows in the Duomo in Arezzo).
- *Annunciation* (Baccio Ciarpi).
- An ancient organ (Caesar and Roman Augustine, 1613).

L'Ermeo di Celle

43.294098, 12.000756
Outside the walls.
Località Le Celle 73
52044 Cortona

Website (Italian): http://www.en.cortonaguide.com/le_celle.html

16 Other Churches in Cortona

Ermeo di Celle.

The convent and hermitage of Le Celle is a Franciscan settlement about a 30-minute walk outside the walls of Cortona hidden in a narrow valley with its buildings climbing Monte Sant'Edigio like steps. It was founded by St. Francis in 1211 and believed to be the place he dictated his will four months before his death in 1226. It was restored in 1969. It is an inspiring, reflective, peaceful place.

There is a small cell behind the chapel believed to be where St. Francis lived when he visited Le Celle. There are now seven friars at Le Celle continuing to practice the teachings of St. Francis and maintaining the facilities. They offer lodging to those thinking of taking to the religious life and to independent groups of visitors.

Saint Francis' cell at the Ermeo di Celle.

It is a gorgeous place to visit and walk around without even going inside. A stream flows down small waterfalls through the valley right next to the cells and chapels.

The Plan of the Fortezza di Girifalco

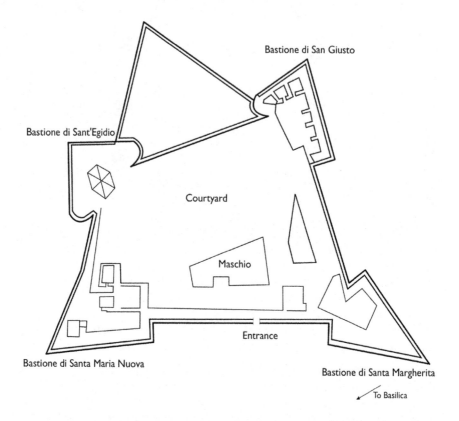

17 Fortezza di Girifalco

Location:

43.276549, 11.993675
Via di Fortezza

0575.1645507
336.2017100

Website: http://www.fortezzadelgirifalco.it (English and Italian)

Email: info@fortezzadelgirifalco.it

Inner courtyard of the Fortezza Girifalco.

"Girifalco" is a large, rare falcon. To get to the fortezza walk up the short trail from the Santuario di Santa Margherita. You can park in the church's parking lot.

Hours:

Opening and closing hours vary depending on events organized at the Fortress. Check the above website for hours. Generally ...

Daily: 10.00-18.00.

Admission: €5.00 to €8.00 depending on the event.

Time to visit: Thirty minutes to walk around. Longer if there is a special art exhibit.

Reasons for a visit: An almost complete medieval fortress with much to explore. There is usually a special art exhibit which is

Fortezza wall.

Ancient printing press on display in the forezza.

worth the price of admission. The views from the highest point of the *fortezza* are spectacular.

Photography: Yes.

Accessibility: Touring the grounds of the castle would be difficult because of soft ground, steep steps, no elevators. However, the areas used for the gallery and cultural events are accessible with ramps and an elevator.

GIRIFALCO

It is a trapezoidal plan with several levels to adapt to the unevenness of the ground above the Basilica di Santa Margherita. From its 651 m above sea level (2136 ft) it gives you the view of a falcon of the Valdichiana to the north to Lago Trasimeno to the south.

The original foundations for the fort were from Etruscan ruins. It was used by the Romans and in the middle ages until sacked in 1258. The modern fortress was rebuilt on ancient ruins in 1549. In 1556, Grand Duke Cosimo I had it connected to the city walls. The reconstruction continued until 1561. There is no evidence that it was attacked after the reconstruction. The bastions of Santa Margherita, Santa Maria Nuova, Sant'Egidio, and San Justino held defensive canon. Each is shaped differently to accommodate the terrain. Only the bastion of Santa Margherita is open for visits. The central body of the castle and its courtyards are open for visitors.

Several of the interior rooms have been remodeled to serve as galleries for the frequent art shows and cultural events. It is also used as a lookout tower for spotting forest fires.

VISITING THE FORTEZZA

You enter the *fortezza* through an old guard room where they sell tickets to the *fortezza* and its special events and exhibits.

From the guard room are new steps to climb. The first stop is a display of an old printing press. More steps lead to the exhibit area.

III Eating, Sleeping, and Events in Cortona

Dolce of sweetened ricotta with fresh strawberry sauce at the Trattoria la Grotta in Cortona.

> *He who has seen one cathedral ten times has seen something; he who has seen ten cathedrals once has seen but little; and he who has spent half an hour in each of a hundred cathedrals has seen nothing at all.*
> Sinclair Louis

A statue honoring the "Idea of Flight" with both da Vinci's "Every man" and Icarus represented. Outside the Chiesa di San Domenico.

18 Sleeping in Cortona

LOCANDA PRETELLA HOTEL 26

43.274371, 11.985751

Vicolo Petrella, 26
52044 Cortona

Graziella's cell: 338.4187837
Land line: 0575.604102
Daily: 10.00-17.00:

Website: https://www.booking.com/hotel/it/locanda-petrella.html

Email: info@petrella26.com

Locanda Petrella occupies three floors of a sixteenth century building in a quiet location in the heart of Cortona. It has five double rooms and two triple rooms, each with bath, shower, AC, TV, mini fridge, and free wifi. All the rooms open onto a spacious salon and breakfast room. A wide staircase with metal balustrades goes to the two rooms on the upper floor.

The rooms are modern with stylish fixtures and comfortable beds integrating the ancient stone structure and massive wooden beams. Towels are the traditional waffled linen, with a bath towel big enough to be a blanket. There is plenty of scalding hot water.

Cell phone reception was good, but for 3G I had to stand by the window.

Graziella is the owner and a gracious, cheerful hostess seeing to your every need. I enjoyed my stay there. Ask for a "deal" if staying more than a couple of days.

BREAKFAST

The breakfast room is also a living room with overstuffed chairs and a large fireplace decorated with prints of modern art around the walls. Two tables take care of the breakfast crowd, or you could enjoy your own picnic lunch there.

Breakfast is an elaborate collection of pastries and breads. There is a toaster. Available to drink are orange juice, *caffè* and hot milk. I was there alone and told her not to bother with breakfast, but she still brought out enough for ten other people.

RUGAPIANA VACANZE

43.2741051, 11.9876848

Via Nazionale, 63
52044 Cortona

Massimo's Cell:
340.8086879

Website: It doesn't have it's own site, use a booking site or call for a reservation.

Email: info@rugapianavacanze.com

"Rugapiana" is the ancient name for car-free Via Nazionale, the only flat street in Cortona and the heart of the historical and tourist center. It's an ideal location for travelers who want to be in the heart of the action with everything a few steps away.

The hotel is an ancient palazzo restored into several rooms and a few apartments with kitchens. Each room integrates the old stone walls, wood beamed ceilings, and terracotta floors, and are furnished with antiques. The TV in my room was also an antique of the old CRT variety.

Rooms are cozy and comfortable with deluxe terry-cloth towels, bathrobes, shower, refrigerator, ceiling fan, and wifi. It has strong wifi though for 3G cell reception I had to stand at the window. The bathrooms are modern and comfortable if not spacious. Soap was a tiny bar, broken into a dozen pieces.

The hotel gives you a voucher for breakfast at any of the local bars on Via Nazionale good for a pastry and cappuccino.

It is a bit less expensive than the Locanda Petrella.

Massimo is helpful, friendly and speaks excellent, rapid English.

Pasta with Fresh Tomatoes

In late summer (in Colorado) there is usually an abundance of fresh tomatoes at the farmers' markets, perfect for this recipe. Well drained tomatoes are important, so after removing the skins squeeze out the seeds, chop coarsely, and then let them drain in a colander to drain while working on the other steps of the recipe. (Store-purchased tomatoes don't need peeling, but they don't taste great either. Use cherry or grape tomatoes instead).

Ingredients

1/2 med sweet onion finely chopped
3 to 4 fresh tomatoes, skinned, seeded, and chopped coarsely
1 t garlic, finely minced
1/4 c EVOO
1/2 t red pepper flakes
4 oz fresh buffalo mozzarella cut into 1/4-inch cubes. Bring to room temperature.
8 oz fresh pasta like penne or rotelli.
3 T fresh grated parmigiano-reggiano
salt and pepper

Directions

- Peel, seed, core, and chop the tomatoes.
- Finely chop 1/2 onion.
- Heat oil in pan over medium low heat, add oil, onion, and hot pepper flakes and sauté gently until onions are transparent and beginning to brown. Then add the garlic and sauté gently for another couple of minutes.
- Heat salted water to boil. Add pasta and cook until al dente.
- About two minutes before the pasta is ready, add the tomatoes to the pan to warm them up so they don't cool the pasta.
- Add about 1/4 c of pasta water to the sauce, then drain pasta.
- Add pasta to the pan and stir to mix well with the tomatoes, then put the pasta in a serving bowl.
- Add the mozzarella pieces and stir and mix well.
- Add the parmigiano. The parmigiano and mozzarella will serve to thicken the sauce.
- Serve with more parmigiano on the side.

19 Eating in Cortona

TRATTORIA LA GROTTA

43.274945, 11.985402
Piazza Baldelli 3
Just off Piazza Repubblica in a tiny alley

0575.630271

Hours: Wed-Mon: 12.00-14.30, 19.00-21.30
Closed Tuesdays

Website: www.trattorialagrotta.it

Contact: Website: www.trattorialagrotta.it/contatti

Simply outstanding.

After my friends and I had finished our tour of the MAEC I stopped at the ticket counter and asked the clerk, in Italian, for a good restaurant, one that she would like to eat at. The clerk gave the standard PC reply, "All of the restaurants in Cortona are good. BUT, I like the Trattoria La Grotta." To add to the reliability of her advice she did not pull out a business card for the restaurant. Whenever a hotel or a tourist site pulls out a business card it means that there is a special "relationship" between the two and not necessarily a great meal.

Trattoria la Grotta is squeezed into a tiny alley next to Piazza Repubblica.

The four of us walked a short distance to have *pranzo*. Sitting inside the door is an antique corker for wine bottles. Inside are two rooms with typical Tuscan beige stone exterior walls and plastered interior walls. A stone and brick arch separates the rooms. Around the 12 tables are book cases

An antipasto of fresh tomatoes, arugula, and burrata cheese.

filled with wine bottles. The owner took us to our table and then came by to take our orders. The pasta is homemade. We had an antipasto of grilled vegetables and *carpaccio* followed by pasta with porcini mushrooms, ravioli, *pici*, and a pork chop topped off with a pudding for dessert.

The next time I returned I made sure that I was starving so I could have a more elaborate meal. Again the owner took me to the table. I asked him for the day's specials and he gave me a handwritten sheet of paper to add to the regular menu — you have to ask, it is only in Italian and kept for locals. I began with an *antipasto* of *burrata* (aka *burratine*) cheese on a bed of peppery arugula with tomato slices and added some olive oil. *Burrata* is a soft and rich combination of mozzarella and cream giving a rich contrast to the bed of bitter arugula.

Top: The primo piatto at Trattoria la Grotta: pici with a cinghiale ragù.
Above: the contorno of grilled eggplant, peppers, and zucchine.

My *primo piatto* was osso bucco in a rich, thick tomato sauce garnished with a couple of bay leaves. The osso bucco is sliced thin but is about six-inches in diameter. It isn't as tender as the braised US method of cooking thick slices but the flavor is intense. My *contorno* was a plate of tender, fresh spring asparagus cooked *al dente* accompanied by a wedge of lemon.

I finished the meal with a *dolce* of sweetened fresh ricotta layered with fresh strawberry sauce in a tall goblet and a *caffè*. It was a smooth ricotta with a creamier texture than we find in the US. The strawberries seemed picked that morning from the garden.

I've had other meals since then and they are always outstanding.

CAFFÉ DEGLI ARTISTI

43.274760, 11.985749
Via Nazionale, 18

0575.601237

Hours:

Daily: 08.00-23.00.

Facebook: https://www.facebook.com/pages/category/Coffee-Shop/Caffè-degli-Artisti-352821811567421/

One of my inviolable rules is "Never ever eat at a restaurant on the main tourist street or piazza. Never."

I'd just spent a morning visiting places in Cortona and had walked up and down the hill twice. It was 2:00 and I was starving so I started walking along the main street looking into the side streets and alleys for a restaurant. As I walked by one place I caught a whiff of black truffle from a plate of spaghetti that a woman was eating. It smelled amazing, but it was on the main drag and violated my rule. I continued to the end of the street and turned around to go back. Again I passed the woman eating spaghetti in truffle sauce. I love truffles! I broke my rule and gave in to both the truffles and hunger and sat down at one of the outside tables squeezing space out of Via Nazionale.

At the Caffè degli Artisti: pasta with black truffle sauce.

I struck up a conversation with the woman eating the truffle pasta. She told me that she ordered it special and that it wasn't on the menu. When the owner came for my order I asked for the same. First, though, I began with bruschetta with prosciutto and melted pecorino cheese. It came on a crispy slice of bread with a thin slice of prosciutto on top of the pecorino. Then came my half order (the full order is huge) of spaghetti with a creamy truffle sauce. Truffles are a rare treat, especially at a reasonable price. Cream is a perfect match with the earthy truffles. I finished with a plate of sliced mixed fruit in season.

It was an excellent meal from a place that looked like an over priced tourist bar on the main tourist street. Far from overpriced, the truffle pasta was only €5.00 ($7.00). Does this mean I will violate my rule with impunity? I don't think so. It's still a pretty good guideline, but I have learned to follow my nose.

RISTORANTE LA LOGGETTA

43.274888, 11.985475
Piazza Pescheria 3, next to Piazza Repubblica.

0575.630575

Hours:

Thur-Tues: 12.00-15.00, 19.00-23.00

Website: http://www.laloggetta.com

Email: info@laloggetta.com

The food is OK, but the main reason to eat here is to sit above Piazza Repubblica under the covered *loggia* or umbrellas and watch the people in the piazza. It's a pleasant atmosphere with plastered walls, attractive tables and dinnerware.

As I said, the food is not great and it costs too much to be mediocre. Their pastas are disappointments with bland sauces and mushy noodles.

Top: the restaurant has outdoor seating under the loggia and umbrellas above Piazza Repubblica.
Above: Antipasto at La Loggetta: crostini nero, salsiccia, pecorino cheese, prosciutto, and bresaola.

However, I've also had a good snack there. I ordered a plate of cured meats, cheese, and bruschetta — a typical Tuscan antipasto. It was served in a unique, attractive way, on a piece of black slate. The problem was that the slate had dulled all the knives in the restaurant and it was impossible to cut the meat. Still, all was fresh and of high quality.

Ristorante Il Cacciatore

43.27515, 11.98487

Via Roma 11/13
0575.613780

Hours:

Mon: 18.00-22.30
Tue-Sun: 12.00-15.00, 18.00-22.30

Email: info@ilcacciatore-cortona.it

Facebook: https://www.facebook.com/ilcacciatorecortona/

Website: https://www.ilcacciatorecortona.it

While on a main street, the restaurant doesn't stand out with a lot of signage, only the name painted in green on the wall. It's one of those small, hidden places frequented by locals known for its excellent food. It has two dining rooms and seating outside in the summer months.

The food is traditional Tuscan fare and specializes in serving Chianina beef, fresh pasta, and seasonal vegetables. The wine selection is extensive.

I recommend this as highly as the Trattoria La Grotta.

Once the travel bug bites there is no known antidote, and I know that I shall be happily infected until the end of my life.
Michael Palin

20 Cortona Events

Giostra dell'Archidado

The crossbow competition is held on the second Sunday in June in Piazza Signorelli. Every year, a procession of more than 300 people wearing medieval costumes march through Cortona's historic center. The crossbow men who come from Cortona's five quarters, or *quartiere*, compete for a golden arrow. The contest originated in 1397 to celebrate the wedding of Francesco Casali and Antonia Salimberi. The festival re-enacts the wedding and the town is festooned with banners.

Website: http://www.giostraarchidado.com/en/.aspx

Tuscan Sun Festival

Last week of July, first week in August. The arts festival celebrates classical music, food, art exhibitions, and alternative medicine. Some of the world's finest musicians, scholars, authors, Academy Award-winners, artists, critics, and historians come to the festival, which also incorporates side events ranging from food and wine tastings to traditional Chinese medicine and fresco-making workshops.

Website: http://www.cortonaweb.net/en/cortona-events/tuscan-sun-festival

SAGRA DI BISTECCA

Middle of August. An outdoor culinary event celebrating the succulent meat from the Valdichiana *chianina* beef. The town cooks *bistecca alla Fiorentina* (steak Florentine) on a 14-meter long (46 ft) super grill — "rare" is the only option. Citizens and visitors line up for steak accompanied by local wines. There are also other exhibits of typical Cortonese products. It costs about €25.00, and includes steak, vegetable, bread, fruit, and wine or water. Held at the Parterre Gardens.

Photos from WMC.

SAGRA DEL FUNGO PORCINO

On the weekend following the *Sagra di Bistecca* the *porcini* mushroom is celebrated. Taste dishes based on mushrooms collected in the hills around Cortona. There are *antipasti, primi piatti, secondi piatti,* and *contorni* — mushroom everything. Served with local wines.

CORTONA ANTIQUARIA

End of August and beginning of September. The prestigious Casali and Vagnotti palaces hold an exhibition of very valuable antiques and artworks. It is a gathering of antique dealers and collectors from all over Italy. It attracts about 20,000 visitors. It has a highly select group of about fifty exhibitors.

Website: http://www.cortonantiquaria.it

IV Information

A Cortona doorway.

Italy, and the spring and first love all together should suffice to make the gloomiest person happy.
Bertrand Russell

Prosciutto slicer at a local festival.

21 Travel Information

WATER, WINE, AND PICNICS

You can save a pile of euros by using grocery stores for essentials. For example, Italians drink bottled water everywhere: homes, restaurants, picnics, etc. Buying water in bars and restaurants is expensive; however, if you visit a grocery store, you can buy water for only a few cents a bottle. Grocery stores also sell expensive and inexpensive wines. You can buy cheap, drinkable wine for as little as €.50 a liter. The grocery stores are also the best places to pick up cured meats, cheese, olives, and salads for picnics at a fraction of the cost that you'd pay at specialized delis. Imagine a lunch for €5.00, saving euros for a special dinner.

A mixed plate of antipasti.

TRANSPORTATION

LOCAL BUSES

Local buses are orange. Tobacco shops (*tabacchi*) and some news kiosks sell tickets. When boarding the bus, enter from the front and look for a small orange box; insert your ticket to validate it. To catch a bus, stand at a bus stop. If a sign says *richeista*, it means that the bus stops only on request, so wave your arms.

TRAVEL AGENTS — AGENZIA

Italians make their plans through travel agents. There are almost as many *Agenzie* as bars. With complicated plans, travel agents will help you find the cheapest tickets, arrange car rentals, and print out all of your tickets and paperwork. For a fee.

INTERCITY BUSES

All the towns in Tuscany have intercity buses. The ticket office is usually near the railroad station. The buses are in excellent condition with air conditioning. Bus tickets are cheaper than a train with most tickets to nearby towns less than €10.00.

Getting Gas

Gas stations close for the afternoon lunch hours and all day Sunday, however, most have self-service pumps. The trick is figuring out how to use the confusing pumps. There is a general pattern. First, drive up to a pump. Second, before using the pump, you find a kiosk, select the number of your pump and pay for the amount of gas you want: €20, €10, or €5. If you want a full tank, you will have to use a pump marked *"servizio,"* "service."

Traveling by Train

Tickets are sold in three ways: online, at a kiosk in the train station, and at the ticket window. Online is convenient and you no longer need a paper ticket. You can download the code to show the conductor. http://trenitalia.com.

- The kiosks in the train stations are great and keep you from long lines. They have an English option. The process begins by selecting your point of departure, then the destination. Then choose first or second class (remember, both first and second class arrive at the same time). Select your seats and the number of tickets needed. Insert the credit card and pay. Don't be in a hurry. The kiosks print slowly and tell you how many cards it is printing. Make sure that you wait for all the cards.
- The ticket window is another option. However, lines move slowly and you'll be fighting your way to the front as little old ladies cut in front of you.
- Reserve your trip online. When finished the site gives you a code for your reservation to show the conductor.

Don't forget to validate the ticket. Find the small red boxes on the way to the track and at the track itself. Insert the ticket and it will print a small code with the date. Conductors don't like it if you forget to validate.

Using the Phone

You can get phone cards for the public phones in the *tabbacchi* shops. Tell the salesperson where you want to call and she will find the best card for calling that locality. Using phone cards is an inexpensive way to call the US, often only about .07 cents (euro) a minute. Though my T-Mobile account only charges .05 cents (US) for voice calls.

Useful phone numbers:

Often an English speaking operator is available.

- Emergency aid services: 113
- Carabinieri: 112
- Fire brigade: 115
- ACI (Automobile Club of Italy): 116. The ACI assistance center can be contacted through the number 06-4477.
- News about motorway traffic conditions can be requested through the number 055-2697.

Clockwise from left: European adapter, USB splitter for charging devices, emergency battery, and European outlet splitter.

Electricity and Battery Charging

(Refers to photo at upper right.)

European electricity runs on 220-volt direct current. All of your battery chargers (made within the last decade or so) will adapt automatically from USA 110 current to European 220 volt. The charger will have "110 to 220 v" written in tiny letters somewhere on the charger. All you will need is an adapter for European wall plugs, see device on the left above.

A problem is that we carry more and more devices that need to be charged, usually with a USB cable. The top device in the picture lets you charge three USB devices at a time. You don't need to bring additional charging "blocks" with you. You can find these chargers with up to 10 USB ports and they work with AC and DC current.

The device on the right is an "emergency" battery. It will charge your phone three times or tablet one to two times.

The object on the bottom is a European splitter for plugging in three different plugs at a time.

Do not go to a travel store to buy the plug adapter. You will usually have to buy several adapters used around the world. You can usually buy the European adapter at a hardware or electronics store in the US or in Italy for a couple of bucks or euros. Get the emergency battery at an electronics store. You can also find any of these on Amazon. (**Note:** The Japan adapter looks a lot like the European plug, but it has thicker prongs.)

INTERNET ACCESS — HOTSPOTS

Most bars and restaurants offer free wifi. The city libraries have computers and free wireless; you'll need your passport to register. Some towns have free wifi from busy parks or piazza, which you sign up for at the official TI office. Hotels almost universally offer free wifi. (Though it seems that the more expensive the hotel the less likely the wifi is free.) As a last resort, you can also purchase a *chiavetta* —a key — that fits into a USB port from one of the phone providers, such as TIM, that links you to the internet; three months is usually the minimum time.

It is slow. The Italian infrastructure for broadband is poor and you will be lucky to find anything faster than 12 mps.

USE YOUR PHONE AS A HOTSPOT

Check with your own cell phone company before you go to see if you can use your cell as a hotspot. I use T-Mobile and often use it to connect because when wifi is unavailable. The speed, though is usually 3G speed. It is rare to get 4G speeds. 5G? Hopefully in my lifetime. Painful.

MEDICAL HELP

If you need a doctor ask your hotel or the TI. There are urgent care centers and hospitals. Your best bet is to head to the hospital emergency ward to find a doctor quickly. Charges will be low, if there are any. I made a trip to the Venice hospital and the emergency cost was €32.00, however they never billed me.

HEALTH INSURANCE

Check your health insurance provider and your credit card benefits before leaving to see if it would be a good idea to purchase additional coverage.

STRIKES (SCIOPERO)

Periodically through the year there are strikes among transportation workers: trains, buses, air traffic controllers, and the like. Sometimes they are for a full day, others for a half day. Pay attention to the news, because the strikes are announced ahead of time.

OVERNIGHT OPTIONS

Hotels are classified by the awarding of stars, from one star for modest facilities up to five for luxury hotels. Camping sites, of which there are thousands, are also classified by a star system, from one to four, according to comfort. As far as free camping is concerned, inquire at the local TI office or research online ahead of time. There are dozens of youth hostels enrolled with AIG (the Italian Youth Hostel Association) spread around the country. The *agriturismo* sector has working farms all over Italy in Trentino-Alto Adige, Veneto, Tuscany, and Apulia. Also use AirBnB.

Finally, there are no longer enough monks and nuns to fill monasteries and convents. Most have opened up as basic hotels to find the money to keep operating. I always stay at the convent of San Giuseppe di Cluny in Rome. To find options go to:

https://www.trails.com/list_2726_canoe-paddling-techniques.html?utm_source=adestra&utm_medium=email&utm_campaign=030918

BANKS, FOREIGN EXCHANGE BUREAUS AND ATMS

Banks are open from 09.00-13.30 and 14.30-16.00, Monday through Friday.

Almost all banks have ATM machines, called **Bancomats**. Using one of these machines will provide the best exchange rates and can save considerable amounts of money and difficulties over the use of Travelers Checks. Do not use your credit card to get cash. The credit card companies charge several fees making it a very bad deal. ATM/Bancomat fees also vary by bank. Deutesche Bank is reasonable.

NUMBERS, COMMAS, AND DECIMALS

When representing quantity, Europeans use a comma as a decimal point, and a decimal point as a comma. For example:

US Figure	European Figure
$25,000	€25.000
$7,000	€7.000
$6.50	€6,50
.25	,25

THE EURO €

The euro consists of coins: .01, .02, .05, .10, .20, .50 cents and 1.00 and 2.00 euros. Bank note denominations include: 5, 10, 20, 50,

100, 500 and 1,000 euros. All of the bank notes are different sizes with different color schemes. Check recent exchange rates online.

BEFORE YOU LEAVE HOME: PACKING

Here's what I take for a two month stay in Italy.

3 shirts (light, quick dry)	1 fleece jacket (early spring or fall)
2 pants (light, quick dry)	1 shorts (summer)
1 black running/walking shoe	1 rain jacket (early spring or fall)
swimsuit or running pants	3 lightweight quick dry underwear
3 pair of socks	wash cloth (doesn't exist in Europe)
toiletries	1 running shirt
camera, iPad, lenses, mic	notebook/journal
maps	guidebooks (tear up)
sleepwear	sewing kit (taken from a hotel)
hat	adapters for electricity and car

- I wash a couple of things every night in the sink. I don't care about wrinkles.
- If it is colder than I expected I'll go to a store (not tourist shop) and buy a sweatshirt.

DOCUMENTS FOR TRAVELING IN ITALY

PASSPORTS

To get a hotel room you will need by law your passport. If you forget it, you'll be sleeping in your car or the train station. If you go into a bank for cash, you will need the passport.

AUTOMOBILES

INTERNATIONAL DRIVERS LICENSE

Many sources recommend an international drivers license, though the information on this card is the same as on your drivers license and passport. I've been driving for over 20 years in Europe and have never bothered with it. If you want one, the AAA issues them — for a fee.

INSURANCE

You cannot rent a car in Italy without paying for liability and theft insurance. It's a good idea. It usually comes with €200.00 deductible. Your risk of minor accidents increases since you are not familiar with the roads and driving laws (written and unwritten).

EMERGENCY BREAKDOWN SERVICES

Emergency breakdown services in Italy are run by ACI (Automobile Club d'Italia). The service operates 24 hours a day throughout the road network.

The Automobile Club d'Italia (ACI) is a public, non-profit organization, which officially represents and defends the general interests of Italian motorists by managing, on behalf of the Italian Government, the Car Public Registry. They also provide technical, road, financial, legal, insurance assistance, and promote car training and drivers education in order to improve the usage of vehicles on the Italian motor ways. On the motor ways breakdown services can be called through the yellow emergency posts located approximately every two km.

TRAFFIC REGULATIONS

Contrary to popular belief, there are speed limits and speed traps (a lot of photo enforcement). In urban areas, it is 50 km/h; on main roads it is 90 to 110 km/h, and 120 km/h on the *autostrada*. (Multiply by .6 to get the equivalent mph: 120 km is a bit over 72 mph.)

- The new highway code recently introduced in Italy following EC directives also stipulates that one must not drive at a speed which is so slow as to hinder the flow of traffic.
- The left lane is used only to pass! This is enforced by both police and drivers. Watch the mirror. A car that looks a long way away will suddenly be behind you flashing its brights — or may bump you. The vehicle being overtaken must maneuver out of the lane and not accelerate.
- Wearing seat belts is the law — front and rear seats.
- Children need child seats.
- Only hands-free cell phone use is permitted while driving.
- A helmet is the law on two wheeled vehicles.
- Flashing of headlights is permitted to signal an intention to overtake.

See my book *Walking the Aqueduct* for more detailed information on driving in Italy, including how to navigate.

OPENING HOURS: SITES, SHOPS, AND RESTAURANTS

Opening hours for museums, churches, and other sites are not uniform. The biggest problems that you will have will be identifying the days that sites are closed and working around the lunch hours.

Most museums and other sites close one day a week. Usually it is Monday or Tuesday. It is generally the same for all sites within a town. Sites in the most popular places like Rome, Venice, Florence, and Pisa are usually open every day and do not close for lunch anymore.

Churches are usually closed during lunch hours.

Opening hours of shops vary from region to region. Shops are usually open from 09.00 to 12.30 and from 15.30/16.00 until 19.00 from Monday to Saturday. They are usually closed on Monday morning.

Restaurants are open for lunch: 11.00/12.00 to 14.00/15.00. Dinner hours are between 19.00 to 22.00. Some open at 20.00. Restaurants usually close one day during the week (not weekends), often Monday or Wednesday. Sometimes a restaurant may be closed on Monday and again for Wednesday lunch, though open for dinner.

POST OFFICE

The post office is open from 08.00-13.30/14.00 from Monday to Friday, and Saturday 08.00-11.45. When you enter a post office you will find a kiosk for receiving a number. There are different kiosks for mailing letters or packages. There will be a light showing the current number being served above the counter.

POLITE CULTURAL PRACTICES WHEN SHOPPING

AT THE STORE

When entering and leaving a small shop, it's customary to greet the shopkeeper with one of the following:

salve (sahl-vay): more formal and much appreciated; can be used for entering and leaving. It is a polite way of saying both "hello" and "goodbye."

buon giorno (bwon jor-no): Good morning. Used before afternoon closing time (around 13:00).

buona sera (bwon-ah sayr-ah): Good afternoon or good evening. Used late afternoon and evening.

arrividerci (ah-reev-ah-dehr-chee): formal goodbye.

If you want to handle the merchandise ask, "*Posso?*" (poh-soh) "May I?" Do not handle without permission.

VEGETABLE AND FRUIT MARKETS

In the small stores, it is impolite to handle the vegetables and fruit. Ask the clerk for what you want (or point) and then she will pick out the best available. To communicate quantity say, "*Vorrei*" (vohr-ay-ee) and hold up fingers to show how much you would like.

Use your thumb to indicate "one." If you hold up your index finger, the clerk will assume that you mean "two."

KINDS OF RESTAURANTS

Traditionally there are five kinds of restaurants, each with its own characteristics. Over the years, these distinctions are becoming more and more blurred.

OSTERIA

The *osteria* specializes in meats cooked over an open wood fire.

TRATTORIA

Less formal than a *ristorante*, it has a full complement of antipasti, *primi, secondi, contorni*, and *dolce* along with pizzas.

RISTORANTE

More expensive and more formal than a *trattoria*, you can count on tablecloths and cloth napkins along with a more specialized menu.

PIZZERIA

Although you can buy pizza in bars and from some storefronts, those pizzas are usually frozen and reheated. A pizzeria makes the pizzas by hand and bakes them in a pizza or wood-fired oven. Pizzas are about twelve-inches in diameter, and the normal practice is to order one pizza per person. It sounds like a lot, but pizzas are cracker thin and use less sauce and cheese than US pizza shops.

TAVOLA CALDA

"Hot table." Cafeteria-style food, fresh and delicious.

AT THE RESTAURANT

In Europe the table is yours for the evening. Italian restaurants don't base their costs on several rapid turnovers. The service is relaxed and acknowledges Italy's belief in "slow food," cooking each dinner individually. You can wile away the evening at your table with your companions.

The waiter, not wanting to rush you, will not deliver your check until you ask for it. Get the waiter's attention and either make a check mark sign with your hand or ask, "*Il conto per favore.*" (il cohn-toh per-fah-vohr-ay), "The bill please."

Waiters often use a wireless, hand held device that processes your chip credit card on the spot.

Basic Courtesies

Using Ciao

Ciao (chow) is an informal way of saying hello and goodbye. Use ciao only with friends and family. For others, say, "*Arrivederci*" (ah-ree-vay-dehr-chee) or *salve* (sal-vay).

Body Language

It is rude to talk with someone with your hands in your pockets.

Smile.

To indicate that something tastes good, put of your index finger against your cheek and rotate back and forth.

Someone may indicate that you should watch for pickpockets and thieves with a gesture that begins with palm and fingers out, and then each finger, starting with the pinkie, folds down into the palm.

To make an emphatic "No!" Raise your hands, stick up your index fingers and make a quick movement back and forth (twice) by crossing and uncrossing your hands with the index fingers pointing up.

One of the most common gestures is shrugging your shoulders straight up, holding your hands out, elbows next to the body, and pouting the lower lip. This has a variety of meanings: "I don't know," "Who cares?" "It doesn't matter," "Bullshit," "What did you expect?" or "Tough luck."

Do NOT point at someone when talking.

Politics

The Italians have no trouble telling you what they believe about Italian and US politics. However, keep your opinions to yourself about both Italy and your own country. It is OK to ask about Italian politics to learn about the country, but avoid a debate. For Italians, debating is a skill learned from the cradle.

STANDING IN LINE

Generally, there are no organized queues in Italy. Keep moving forward, protect your sides and use your elbows. If you wait calmly, you'll still be waiting an hour later. When you get to the front of the line, protect your flanks. It's common for someone to come up beside you and cut in front — usually old ladies. It helps for two people together to wait in the line, then you can protect both flanks.

SHHHH

Talk in tones that match the place you are at. Be courteous. If someone does not understand, talking louder doesn't help.

HUMOR

The subtlety of humor doesn't translate well, especially sarcasm and irony. Avoid it.

BEING A GUEST

When invited to someone's home, don't be in a hurry. Dinner may begin between 20:00 and 21:00. Don't rush; they expect you to stay until midnight. If you want to take something to your hosts, take flowers, chocolates, or wine.

Try everything that is served. Not only is the dinner usually four to five courses, each course will often have more than one option. For example, the *secondo* may include *bistecca*, rabbit, chicken, and sausage. The *antipasti* may have three to six options.

Eat slowly because when your plate is empty, the host will fill it again. The best defense is to match the pace of your hosts and finish the course when they do.

For more information on the art of dining, especially as a guest, see my book *Walking the Aqueduct*.

PUSHY PUSHY

The Italians are forthright; sometimes they seem pushy. They will ask personal questions out of the blue. "How much did that cost?" "What are you paying for your car rental?" "How much is the hotel?" It's disarming, but doesn't demand an answer. A simple, "Too much!" is fine and they'll back off.

COMPORTMENT IN CHURCHES

- Dress appropriately, pants or shorts should extend below the knee.

- Cover the shoulders.
- Turn off phones.
- Only take pictures when permitted.
- Do not visit during liturgical services.

Lake Trasimeno (horizon line) in the distance from the battlements of the Fortezza Girifalco.

22 Wine Tasting in Italy

TASTING PROTOCOLS

Visiting local Tuscan wineries is a fun way to learn about local wines. However, touring and sampling wines at Italian wineries is different than touring wineries in the USA.

There are some big wine estates in southern Tuscany, such as Castello Banfi near Montalcino, Avignonesi near Montepulciano, and Castello Brolio north of Siena in Chianti. The larger wineries are usually open every weekday and have tasting rooms and vineyard tours in English. However, free wine tastings are a thing of the past. There is usually a small fee for the wines based on the number and variety of wines. As in the USA, visitors are welcome in the tasting rooms at these large operations without appointments. If you want an English tour of the *cantina* where they make wine and of the vineyard, reservations are a must so call ahead or use the winery's website to make reservations.

The old fashioned way. A pruning shears and bucket and you are ready to go.

The majority of Tuscan wineries are small-scale family run operations. They do not have the staff, time, or money to deal with drop-in visitors, especially during harvest time in September and October. You can make reservations on websites, by calling ahead, or by using the Tourist Information service in local towns. For example, in Greve in Chianti

The new way, a machine harvests the grapes by pulling the individual grapes off the bunch. It harvests both sides of a row at once and replaces at least 15 people.

the TI has a map pointing out local vineyards and will help you make a reservation for a tasting.

TASTING

When arriving at the vineyard you will usually be met by a family member who will take you around the farm to look at the operation. Then, they will take out some vintages that they are proud of to offer. In Italy it is courteous to buy a bottle or two from the family-run producers — they are taking valuable time from their day to welcome you.

Larger wineries give you a variety of tastings from their vintages, however there is usually only one or two that would come from the best wines over the years. What you taste also depends on how knowledgeable and interested you seem. The wine makers get excited when they have customers who know what is involved in wine production.

In Montalcino and Montepulciano, there are several *enoteche* (singular is *enoteca*) — wine shops — along the streets where you can find excellent wines to taste, either for free or a small price. The Contucci winery on the Piazza Grande in Montepulciano still offers free tastings.

The shops and wineries may also have *digestivi* to taste, such as *vin santo, limoncello,* and grappa. *Digestivi* are highly alcoholic drinks that Italians serve after the meal in thimble full amounts to help with your digestion. Sounds strange but it works for me. V*in santo* — holy wine — is a treasure (not highly alcoholic). It's made from late harvested grapes that have been left on the vines to dry almost to raisins to be high in sugar. The grapes are crushed leaving a sweet syrupy liquid to make into wine. There is little juice left in a raisin so *vin santo* is expensive, particularly in the USA where a 250 ml bottle will cost thirty dollars or more.

Grappa is an acquired taste that I haven't acquired. It is made by fermenting the stems and skins from wines after they have been crushed. It is a high proof drink that reminds me of the smell of kerosene, though lemon flavored grappa from the freezer is not bad.

A source to examine for wineries is the website "A Self-Guided Wine Tour of Southern Tuscany: Where to Dine, Buy and Sip Wine in Montepulciano and Montalcino" by Richard Marcis: http://www.winewordswisdom.com/.

Wines made by the La Striscia Winery in Arezzo. La Striscia is also an agriturismo.

Training the Grapes

To use the harvester the grapes are trained to grow in a single row below the foliage. The bunches hang down below the leaves. The leaves are trimmed to the height necessary to permit the harvester to go down the rows.

Grape Harvesting

Most of the older generation will tell you that the mechanical harvesting of grapes is an abomination, a crime against the grapes.

Having watched the harvester in action, it does a pretty good job. The grapes are not damaged despite the fact that most of the grapes are removed individually from the stems.

It's also faster than humans. Grapes need to be harvested at their peak and the machine narrows that window of time when the wines are exposed to oxygen improving quality. It moves down the rows at a fast walk harvesting grapes from both sides of the row at the same time.

The Enoteca

The best and easiest way to taste a number of wines at the same time is at an *enoteca*. This *enoteca* is in Greve in Chianti operated by the Falorni family.

The wines are arranged a dozen to a kiosk. The varieties are expansive with Chianti, Vino Nobile, Brunello, grappa, limoncello, super tuscans, whites, and sweet wines. You buy a cash card and use it to choose a wine in each kiosk. The wines are priced from as little as a euro for a taste to €10.00.

Below a taster, my wife Jill, holds her glass for a taste of cold limoncello.

23 Decoding Religious Art

It is often difficult to appreciate paintings, statues, and frescoes beyond thinking, "That's nice;" however, it is easy to learn some basics of art appreciation that will enhance your viewing of religious art (most art in Italy) from the tenth through seventeenth centuries.

THEMES

MULTIPLE STORIES — BACK STORIES

> **Gothic Art**
>
> Gothic art was a medieval art movement developed in France after Romanesque art generally from the mid-twelfth and mid fifteenth centuries, coinciding with the development of Gothic architecture. Painting evolved from stiff two-dimensional forms to more realistic ones.

Paintings were meant to tell stories to the illiterate population, making Christian ideas and events concrete. Artists put expensive canvas space to good use and included more details about the main topic in the background. After your first look at a painting, look again for "multiple frames" — the back stories that offer more information. Examine who is in the background and what is happening. Pay attention to the edges and corners.

Madonna and Child, Lorenzetti, 14th c. This Gothic painting reveals the gold background, awkward body positions and elongated features such as nose, fingers, and eyes.

ARTISTS' PATRONS

A patron often sponsored works of art. For example, the Medici supported young Michelangelo as he carved his David. It was a common practice to insert images of the patrons as one or more of the minor figures in the story.

GOTHIC GOLD AND PERSPECTIVE

A feature of Gothic painting from the eleventh to fourteenth centuries was a gold background representing holiness, and the supernatural. Perspective at this time was crude. Figures appear flat with elongated features, especially the hands and fingers. However, this did not take away from the impact of the paintings, which are often powerful and detailed tellings of Christian events.

Cimabue's Gothic Crucifix, 1270, in the Basilica di San Domenico in Arezzo. Note the liberal use of gold (the light areas outlining the cross). (WGA)

GOTHIC CRUCIFIX

The Gothic crucifix also shows the shortcomings of poor perspective, typical for the thirteenth century. It shows Christ on the cross with elongated limbs and torso. Without good perspective skills, to show the head hanging down, artists painted the head on a separate slanted piece of wood and attached it on an angle to the cross. Each end of the cross has a small rectangle, usually with St. John the Evangelist on one side and Mary on the other. At the top is the Sacred Heart of Jesus, or the Risen Christ. Occasionally there is a rectangle at the bottom with Mary Magdalen.

ANNUNCIATION

The Annunciation shows Mary receiving God's request from Angel Gabriel to be Christ's mother. Mary is either kneeling or sitting with a book (there weren't bound books in Mary's time) on the right side of the painting. The angel is on the left conveying God's request, often holding lilies, a sign of Mary's purity. Here, God's grace shines in gold from the upper left. God is shown above the central pillar, The dove representing the Holy Spirit is just above the angel's head next to the pillar. On the left side of the painting Adam and Eve are being shown out of the Garden of Eden after embracing sin. This recognizes Mary's role in conquering sin by bearing the Christ Child.

The Annuciation by Fra Angelico, 1430, now in the Prado Museum in Madrid. (WGA)

ASSUMPTION AND THE SACRED BELT (GIRDLE)

Mary's Assumption into heaven shows her in the top part of a painting or sculpture. Usually, at the bottom, apostles and saints are standing around an

empty tomb with flowers, looking up in amazement.

According to a medieval legend, the Madonna, near the end of her earthly life, receives a second visit from the Archangel Gabriel. He tells her of her coming death and reunion with her son, Jesus. She expresses her strong desire to her son again.

The apostles, spread throughout the world preaching the gospel, are gathered up by a cloud and carried miraculously to the Virgin Mary in the Valley of Giosafat. Thomas, though, is missing.

Though far away Thomas was able to watch Mary being taken to Heaven. Unaware that the others are also witnesses he asks Mary for a sign to show them and she gives him the belt (*cintola*) from around her dress.

The Assumption by della Robbia, 1500s, in the Sanctuary of La Verna. Mary hands Thomas her sacred belt to prove that she has left the tomb for heaven. (WGA)

THE DEPOSITION OR PIETÀ

The Deposition may portray several things after Christ's death: his removal from the cross, laying in Mary's lap (the pietà), or being laid into the tomb. The classic Pietà is Michelangelo's (1499) shown here in St. Peter's Basilica.

Michelangelo's Pietà in St. Peter's Basilica in the Vatican.

GOD'S ARROWS

When God shows up in a painting he sometimes holds three arrows representing the three theological virtues of Faith, Hope, and Charity. God directly infuses these three virtues into the soul where they help believers live as God's children and merit eternal life.

IMMACULATE CONCEPTION

This is an often misunderstood tenet of Catholic teaching. The Immacu-

The Immaculate Conception, Luca Signorelli, 1523, Museo Diocesano in Cortona. (WGA)

late Conception is not the conception of Christ in Mary's womb at the Annunciation, rather it is Mary's conception in the womb of her mother, St. Anne. Catholic doctrine states that from the first moment of her existence Mary was preserved by God from Original Sin and filled with sanctifying grace.

Interpreting paintings of the Immaculate Conception is difficult because they are highly detailed symbolic allegories. (I don't understand most of it.) However, there are some common elements:

- The importance of Mary is emphasized by her stepping upon and crushing satan (a snake or dragon), symbolizing her role in conquering sin and death. Michael the Archangel may be around to help.
- God the Father and the Holy Spirit (dove) at the top of the painting represent His favor and trust in Mary.
- Lilies and roses are signs of Mary's purity.
- The moon under her feet and twelve stars surrounding her head are possibly a reference to "a woman clothed with the sun" (Revelation 12:1-2).
- Adam and Eve are represented in ways that show their rescue from the grasp of sin by the soon to be born Christ.
- Additional imagery may include clouds, a golden light, angels, saints, and cherubs.

MARY'S ATTIRE

The Holy Mother usually wears a blue robe over a white or red gown. The robe and gown may be solid or patterned, sometimes with gold accents.

MARIA MISERICORDIA

The Misericordia is a depiction of the Blessed Virgin Mother as the Mother of Mercy. Throughout the Middle Ages and Renaissance people looked upon the Holy Mother as an intercessor who helped send their prayers to God. Mary is in the center of the picture, her arms spread, and the outer robe open, usually held by angels. Beneath her robe are her supplicants, the people praying to her for help, often segregated by gender with men on her right and women on the left. Why segregated? I don't know. The Misericordia is portrayed in hundreds of paintings, frescoes, and sculptures.

MULTIPLE MARYS AT THE CRUCIFIXION (THREE MARYS)

The Three Marys refers to a set of three or more women mentioned in the New Testament considered to have been pious followers of Christ. The name "Mary" was common in the Old Testament.

Two of the Marys are obvious: Mary, Christ's mother, and Mary of Magdalen. Scholars don't agree on the third Mary and it may have been Mary of Bethany, Mary Salome the Disciple, Mary mother of James the Less, Mary of Cleopas, Mary of Rome, or Mary, mother of John Mark of Jerusalem. Another factor confusing the issue is that there may have been one set of Marys at the cross, another at the entombment, and still another at the empty tomb.

Above: Typical Misericordia (15th c.).

Below: The Multiple Marys at the Crucifixion.

SEVEN SORROWS OF MARY

Some statues show Mary with seven arrows piercing her breast symbolizing her most sorrowful events:

Seven Sorrows of Mary. (Syrio, WMC)

- *Prophecy of Simeon.* When Mary and Joseph took the Child Jesus to the temple to fulfill the law, Simeon met them and told Mary that Christ's future suffering would be like a sword piercing her heart.
- *Flight to Egypt.* The Holy Family fled in fear when an angel told Joseph to go to Egypt to protect Christ from the "Slaughter of Innocents" by King Herod.
- *Loss of the Child Jesus.* This represents the dread that Mary felt when she realized that the twelve-year old son was not with them after a trip to Jerusalem. Joseph and Mary found him teaching in the temple in Jerusalem a few days later.
- *Mary meets Jesus carrying His Cross* and sees his body covered in wounds.
- *Crucifixion.* She sees her Son nailed to the cross.

St. Francis receiving the stigmata, Gentile de Frabriano, 1453. (WMC, www.aiwaz.net)

- *Mary receives the Body of Jesus* from the Cross.
- *Body of Jesus is Placed in a Tomb.* She gazes for the last time upon her son and the entrance to the tomb is sealed.

"School of" — "Workshop of" — "Studio of"

Each of these phrases describes works of art started by a master and then given to apprentices to complete. For example, the school of della Robbia produced hundreds of ceramic bas-reliefs, thanks to the help of workers and apprentices. The studio of Luca Signorelli produced more paintings than the master could do alone. As the master guided his workers they learned his style.

Stigmata

The holiest of saints receive the stigmata, the wounds of Christ in their hands, feet, and side. The most recent saint with the stigmata was St. Father Pio in Italy in the late 20th century.

Vatican II Altar

One of the results from the Second Vatican Council (Vatican II) was to move the altar from the back of the apse out front so the priest could face the people during Mass. Most altars couldn't be moved, so a new altar, usually a simple table, was placed at the front of the apse — the Vatican II altar.

The Visitation

Mary's cousin Elizabeth was beyond child bearing years, yet through a miracle became pregnant with John the Baptist a few months before Mary became pregnant. Mary went to help her cousin through her final months and Elizabeth greeted with "Hail Mary, full of grace and blessed is the fruit of your womb." Mary leans to bring Elizabeth from her knees.

Saints and Their Symbols

Religious paintings include saints who are difficult to identify without some clues. It's not as hard as it looks because saints are associated with specific symbols.

The Visitation by Vasari, 1500s, in the Badia delle Sante Flora e Lucilla in Arezzo.

Gothic version St. Francis from the 13th c. Museo Civico, Montalcino.

THE PALM BRANCH

Martyred saints often hold a small palm branch (don't confuse it for a feather) symbolizing their holiness and martyrdom.

SYMBOLS OF THE EVANGELISTS

St. Mark is the lion. St. John, the eagle. St. Luke, the ox. St. Matthew, an angel or human.

SANT'AGATA — ST. AGATHA

St. Agatha was a Sicilian from a rich, important family. At a young age she dedicated her life to God and resisted men who wanted to marry or have sex with her. One powerful man, Quintian, had her arrested and told her that she would face torture and death if she did not surrender herself to him. But, she affirmed her belief in God, so he imprisoned her in a brothel. Quintian moved her to prison and tortured her, having her breasts cut off before he killed her. In paintings she is shown holding a plate holding her breasts and a scissors — I don't think that that makes her the patron saint of seamstresses.

SANT'ANTONIO DI PADOVA

St. Anthony's symbol is his tongue to represent the power of his preaching. Anthony is buried in a chapel within the large basilica built to honor him in Padova, Italy. His tongue is displayed for veneration in a large reliquary. The tongue was placed there when his body was exhumed thirty years after his death and it still glistens and looks as if it was still alive — actually, it takes a bit of imagination to accept the "glistening" and "as good as new" claims. So what else would they do but cut it out and place it in a reliquary? In paintings and statues he is portrayed holding his tongue on a plate.

SAN DOMENICO — ST. DOMINIC

St. Dominic was the prior of the order of Dominicans. He preached to heretics and converted barbarians. He is patron saint of astronomers and is depicted with a black robe over a white gown, tonsure, book, and lilies. The Dominicans were the prime movers of the Inquisition (12th to 14th centuries).

SAN FRANCESCO — ST. FRANCIS

St. Francis is easy. He is dressed in a brown robe with a tonsure. Sometimes there are animals around, representing his love for all living things. Another popular depiction shows him on his knees, arms extended and looking toward heaven as spears of light come down and give him the stigmata. He is very popular in Tuscany and almost every town has a church named for him.

SAN GIOVANNI EVANGELISTA — ST. JOHN THE EVANGELIST

The apostle John, "The one Jesus loved," is shown present at the crucifixion. He may hold a pen and book representing his gospel. In many paintings, such as Leonardo's Last Supper, he is clean shaven with long blond hair, a bit effeminate. There may be an eagle, his symbol, or a chalice in the picture. The chalice represents an attempt to poison him. When he lifted the cup, the poison emerged as a serpent.

SAN GIOVANNI BATTISTA — ST. JOHN THE BAPTIST

St. John the Baptist was the son of Mary's cousin, Elizabeth, born a few months before Christ, the second cousin of Christ. St. John's mission was to herald the coming of the Messiah. He is shown as an adult, baby, or child. He usually has bare legs and chest or wears a hair shirt. Other symbols are a cross with double horizontal pieces and a lamb. He often shows up as a child or baby with the child Jesus and the Holy Mother.

Mary Magdalen. Piero della Francesco (15th c.) in the Arezzo Duomo.

SAN GIUSEPPE — ST. JOSEPH

St. Joseph, Mary's husband and Christ's stepfather, always seems to be an old man with a balding pate of gray hair and a beard. Believed to be a carpenter, there are often tools in the paintings.

SAN LORENZO — ST. LAWRENCE

St. Lawrence was martyred by barbecue. He was placed on a grate over a fire. Legend has it that he told his killers, "I believe that I'm done on this side, you can turn me over."

Fresco of St. Peter in Santa Maria in Gradi in Arezzo.

La Maddalena — St. Mary Magdalen

La Maddalena was one of several women who followed Christ. Contrary to legend, the Bible does not describe her as a prostitute. She was more likely a rich person who came to Christ to have her sins forgiven and then became a disciple. She introduced herself by interrupting a dinner and proceeded to wash Christ's feet with her tears, dry them with her hair, and anoint them with expensive oil. She is one of the figures at the crucifixion. Mary, the Holy Mother, wears a blue robe, so Mary Magdalen wears robes of different colors. To represent her washing and anointing of Christ's feet, you'll often see her with a jar of oil and wet hair.

San Michele Arcangelo — St. Michael the Archangel

St. Michael is God's "enforcer." He wears battle armor with a drawn sword standing on a serpent or dragon, representing the defeat of the devil.

San Paolo — St. Paul

Before St. Paul was Paul, he was Saul, a Jew who persecuted the early Christians. Saul saw the light and became Paul, the leading evangelist of the time and writer of a number of epistles. In fact, his epistles were written before the gospels and are the earliest record of the development of Christian communities. He holds a sword representing his role as a soldier of Christ.

San Pietro — St. Peter

Peter is the "rock" upon which Christ founded the church and the first pope. Christ gave Peter, figuratively, the keys to heaven, so he holds keys in paintings. Other symbols include the pope's mitre and crucifix (he was martyred by being crucified upside down).

San Rocco (Roco, Roch)

Patron saint of prisoners, victims of the bubonic plague, and other contagious diseases. A dog is usually in the painting because when he had the plague and was secluded in a cave, the dog kept him alive by bringing bread to him each day. He also has a wound in his leg and holds a staff with a banner.

St. Scholastica

The depiction of St. Scholastica is a bit odd. She is usually a part of another painting, a small character, kneeling in the lower right corner in a black habit with her arms spread. A light comes from heaven illuminating her. There are usually a dove and lilies in the picture. She was the twin sister of St. Benedict.

San Sebastiano — St. Sebastian

An early saint and martyr killed during the Roman Emperor Diocletian's persecution of Christians (ca. 288). He is depicted tied to a tree and shot through with arrows. The arrows didn't kill him so he was clubbed to death.

San Stefano — St. Stephen

St. Stephen is considered the first martyr, stoned to death in Jerusalem shortly after Christ's death. His symbols are stones and a deacon's robe.

San Tommaso — St. Thomas

The phrase "doubting Thomas" applies because he said that he would not believe that Christ had resurrected without placing his hands in Christ's wounds. Mary, at her Assumption, gave Thomas her belt to prove to the other apostles that she had been assumed into heaven. Martyred by sword.

The Mystic Weddings of the St. Catherines

The "wedding" refers to visions of St. Catherine of Alexandria and St. Catherine of Siena. Both dreamed that she was a bride of Christ and woke up with His ring on her finger. After refusing to marry a Roman emperor, Catherine of Alexandria was condemned to death — to be broken on the wheel. However, when she touched the wheel it broke, so she was beheaded instead. The wheel and sword are symbols. She is patron saint of places of education, science, philosophy, and diseases of the tongue.

St. Catherine of Siena was one of the most brilliant theological minds of her day. She received the stigmata, her symbol, after her death. She also wears the crown of thorns.

The Mystic Wedding of St. Catherine, Gio Zelotti, 1547. (WGA)

Church Classifications

Basilica

A basilica is a church building that has been accorded special privileges by the pope. There are two kinds: major and minor. The world's four major basilicas are St. John Lateran, St. Peter's, St. Paul Outside the Walls, and Santa Maria Maggiore, all in Rome.

Minor basilicas are significant churches in Rome and elsewhere in the world that meet certain criteria such as historical, architectural and artistic value.

Duomo — Cattedrale (Cathedral)

A large church in a town that has a bishop, sometimes called a basilica. Cortona and Arezzo have both a basilica and duomo.

Pieve — Parish Church

A large church with a baptismal font and civic focal point in a city without a bishop. Towns with duomos may also have a pieve, like the Pieve della Santa Maria in Arezzo.

Mendicante — Mendicant

A large, plain church with a single nave built by a religious order, especially associated with churches dedicated to San Francesco and San Domenico.

Badia or Abbazia — Abbey

A church owned and operated by an abbey, generally large, and could be rural or urban. Monasteries often had support from wealthy communities and their churches are large and decorated with frescoes, paintings, and sculpture. Two beautiful examples are the Abbazia di Sant'Antimo and the Abbazia di Monte Oliveto Maggiore.

MONASTERO — MONASTERY

Built by a religious order, usually plain with a single nave. The churches of San Domenico in both Arezzo and Cortona were once monasteries.

ORATORIO (ORATORY) OR CHAPEL

A small, privately owned chapel often built by wealthy patrons, such as the one in the Vasari house or at Castello Brolio. Used primarily for prayer and as a site to bury family members.

A polyptych altarpiece by Pietro Lorenzetti, 1320, in the Pieve della Santa Maria in Arezzo. Triptychs and polyptychs are some of the grandest works of art from the 14th and 15th centuries full of characters and stories. Here the bottom panels depict Saints Donato (patron saint of Arezzo), John the Evangelist, Virgin and Child, John the Baptist, and Matthew. The other characters are apostles. The dual center panel shows the Annunciation and the at the top is the Risen Christ.

Relics of Saints

Relics are objects associated with saints. The word relic comes from the Latin word *reliquiae*, meaning "remains." A container used to hold a relic is a "reliquary." Some people and churches keep relics as a reminder of a patron saint. Others believe they have miraculous powers, however the Church does not teach that relics hold special powers. There are three different classes of relics:

First class: An actual part of the saint's body, or the whole body like Santa Margherita in the Santuario di Santa Margherita in Cortona and Sant'Agnese in Montepulciano. Catholics aren't the only group keeping remnants of bodies, witness the preservation of Lenin in Moscow.

Second class: An article of clothing or something the saint used during his or her lifetime. Most relics are of this nature.

Third class: Any object that is touched by a first class relic. Most are small pieces of cloth.

The Vatican rarely confirms the authenticity of these objects. There are probably enough relics of the True Cross around to build three of them. The Catholic Church claims ownership of all relics, possession by an individual are simply "loaners."

During the Middle Ages people made money, the sin and crime of simony, by selling relics such as the nails of Christ, straw from the manger, or cloths with his image.

24 Author: Scott Tiezzi Grabinger

THE WRITER

After I retired from my professorship at the University of Colorado I began thinking about what to do next. I asked myself, "What do I know?" The answer was Arezzo and Tuscany so I began a series of guidebooks.

No one needs another book about Florence, Siena or Pisa. Instead, I focus on the repeat visitor and slow traveler. I take the readers to the small hill towns, local restaurants, *sagre*, markets, and festivals that the first time visitor never sees.

WHAT MAKES MY BOOKS UNIQUE?

1. EXPERIENCE

My family and I have been traveling around Italy since 1992 learning the towns, sites, foods, language, and culture. I stay in Tuscany about two months a year and have made many friends and found even more relatives.

Scott Tiezzi Grabinger author of the "Inside Tuscany: A Second Time Around" guidebook series and "Walking the Aqueduct." (Photo by Beth Joyce.)

2. SLOW TRAVEL.

I describe places that most guidebooks cover in 30 words or less — if at all. To me, second time visitors want to travel slower to engage more in the culture and with the people. Whereas the goal of the first time visitor is to "collect" as much as they can in a few short days leaving little time to taste the *caffè* or gelato.

3. FAMILY MAKES ALL THE DIFFERENCE.

My cousins give me a unique perspective from other writers. They show me the real "Inside Tuscany" with its hidden tiny hill towns, incredible scenery, and pizzerias and restaurants popular to locals. They have taken me to *sagre* (festivals dedicated to a single food like steak, porcini mushrooms, or *ciaccia*) and weekend long festivals and antique fairs. They try to teach me how to "act Italian;" but I still find it hard to get used to eating dinner at 8:30 at night.

4. I speak Italian.

On my first visit I found that only one of my cousins spoke English so I began to learn it. (Later I would find that they'd rather listen to my poor Italian than speak English.) It's impossible to recall the number of times a church caretaker or museum docent have opened up and taken me along on a private 40 minute tour because I could understand. Or the number of times I learned about specialties in a restaurant that aren't on the menu or found the perfect Vino Nobile for the *secondo piatto*, because I could talk to the waiter.

5. I live in Arezzo two months a year.

I live in Tuscany about two months a year. My base is in Arezzo and from there I branch out to discover new places and events, participate in festivals and daily markets, and walk in the evening *passeggiata*, and make friends.

Guide Work and Itinerary Planning

When I'm on site in Arezzo I serve as an unofficial guide for people wanting to visit the local areas. Mostly this includes relatives and friends — who don't pay. I'm also available to advise you on your travel plans. For travel ideas visit www.insidetuscanytours.com.

Don't miss "Walking the Aqueduct"

Now available, a book of true stories about my adventures, misadventures and insights of traveling in Italy: *Walking the Aqueduct: Tuscan Adventures and Culture*.

The book is available in both paperback and Kindle formats from Amazon.com.

Social Media Contacts

When I'm not on site I help people with planning itineraries for their trips to Central Tuscany. Just contact me for help:

Email: scott.grabinger@gmail.com
Facebook: www.facebook.com/scott.grabinger
LinkedIn: www.linkedin.com/in/scott-grabinger-3890b073
Photo Galleries: www.stgimages.com
Book information go to: www.stgbooks.com

Contact Information

8268 East Long Place
Centennial, CO 80112-2609
USA

USA Cell Phone: 303-875-4379

Email: Scott.Grabinger@gmail.com
Facebook: www.facebook.com/scott.grabinger
Website for Books: www.stgbooks.com
Photo Galleries: www.stgimages.com
Tour information about Tuscany: www.insidetuscanytours.com

Occupations

- Travel Writer
- Associate Professor Emeritus, University of Colorado Denver

Camera

- Nikon Z6

Favorite Vacation Spots

- Tuscany
- Colorado Mountains and Colorado Trail
- Boundary Waters Canoe Area and Quetico Superior National Park
- Northwest USA
- France

Languages

- Native English Speaker
- Italian

Hobbies

- Writing
- Photography
- Reading
- Studying Italian
- Building things
- Backpacking

L'Ermeo di Celle gardens. The hermitage is located outside the Cortona walls.

25 Index

A

acquacotta 27
Annunciation 144
art themes
  Annunciation 144
  backstory 143
  God's arrows 145
  Gothic Crucifix 144
  Gothic gold 143
  Immaculate Conception 145
  Maria Misericordia 147
  palm branch 150
  sacred belt 144
automobiles
  emergencies 131
  insurance 130
  traffic regulations 131

B

banks and ATMs 129
basic courtesies 134
  being a guest 135
  body language 134
  ciao 134
  humor 135
  pushy pushy 135
  shhhh 135
  standing in line 134, 135
  talking politics 134
  using ciao 134
Beato (Fra) Angelico 57
broccoli e fagiolini 32
bucchero pottery 35, 44
buses 125

C

Caffé degli Artisti 117
Campianto sul Christo Morto 61
changing money 129
chiaroscuro 65
Chiesa della Santa Maria Nuova 104
Chiesa di Sant'Antonio Abate 103
Churches
  Chiesa della Santa Maria Nuova 104
  Chiesa di Sant'Antonio Abate 103
  Ermeo Le Celle 104
  Le Celle 105

Communion of the Apostles 62
comportment in churches , 13
contact information 159
Cortona Antiquaria 122
costs 12
courtesies 134
Crano 25
cultural practices
  at the restaurant 133
  at the store 132
  vegetable and fruit markets 133

D

Decoding Art and Saints' Symbols
  Mary Magdalene 152
  Mystic Weddings of the St. Catherines 153
  San Michele Arcangelo 152
  San Paolo 152
  San Pietro 152
  San Rocco 152
  San Sebastiano 153
  San Stefano 153
  St. John the Baptist 151
  St. John the Evangelist 151
  St. Joseph 151
  St. Scholastica 153
Descriptions of Churches 14
digestivi 138
documents for traveling in Italy 130
dormice 39

E

electricity 127
encaustic 48
Ermeo Le Celle 104

F

floor counting 13
Franciscans of the Third Order 55

G

gas 126
Giostra dell'Archidado 121
glirarium 39
God's arrows 145
Gothic Art 143
Gothic Crucifix 144
Gothic Gold 143

Grabinger 157

H

Hotels
　Locanda Pretella Hotel 111
　Rugapiana Vacanze 112

I

Immaculate Conception 145
incorrupt remains 93
international drivers license 130
internet access 128
itinerary planning 158

J

John the Baptist 151

K

kinds of restaurants 133
　osteria 133
　pizzeria 133
　ristorante 133
　tavola calda 133
　trattoria 133

L

Lamentation Over the Dead Christ 61
lampadario 41
Le Celle 105
legends of Cortona 25
Legends of Cortona 25
lemon cake 96
Locanda Pretella Hotel 111

M

Madonna Orante 41
MAEC
　glirarium 39
　Musa Polimnia 48
Maria Misericordia 147
Mary Magdalene 152
Marzocco 30
Maternità 45
medical help 128
Musa Polimnia 48
Mystic Weddings of the St. Catherines 153
mythology
　satyrs 40
　sirens 40

N

Noah 25

numbers and decimals 129

O

opening and closing hours 13
opening hours 131
osso bucco 10

P

packing 130
Palazzo Comunale 29
passports 130
pasta water 16
pasta with fresh tomatoes 114
phone 126
photography practices 14
Piazza Signorelli 31
pizzeria 133
Post Office 132
Principle 1: Go slow and easy. Plan to return. 17
Principle 2: Adapt and learn new things. 17
Principle 3: Travel cheap. 17
Principle 4: Come to "tour" and to "live." 17
Principle 5: Put your camera down and look around. 18
Principle 6: Fly under the radar. 18
Principle 7: Does €25.00 really matter? 18
Principle 8: Pack light, walk easy. 18

Q

QR-Codes 13

R

recipe information 15
recipes
　acquacotta 27
　broccoli e fagiolini 32
　chocolate mousse 76
　lemon cake 96
　osso bucco 10
　pasta with fresh tomatoes 114
　veal cutlets 88
Relic of the True Cross 86
relics of saints 156
restaurants
　osteria 133
　pizzeria 133
　ristorante 133
　tavola calda 133
　trattoria 133
Restaurants
　Caffè degli Artisti 117

Ristorante La Loggetta 118
Trattoria La Grotta 115
ristorante 133
Ristorante La Loggetta 118
Roman sarcophagus 54
Rugapiana Vacanze 112

S

Sacred Belt 144
Sagra del Fungo Porcino 122
Sagra di Bistecca 122
saints and symbols 149
San Francesco 150
San Lorenzo 150
San Rocco 152
Santa Margherita 91
satyrs 40
Severini 65, 74, 90, 98, 103
Signorelli 60, 61, 62, 97, 98
Signorelli Hall 60
Signorelli, Luca 61
sirens 40
standing in line 135
St. John the Evangelist 151
St. Joseph 151
St. Michael the Archangel 152
St. Paul 152
St. Peter 152
strikes (sciopero) 128
St. Scholastica 153
St. Sebastian 153
studio of 149

T

time: 24-Hour Clock 13
tips for visiting Tuscan wineries
  tasting 138
train travel 126
transportation 125
  getting gas 126
  intercity buses 125
  local buses 125
  train 126
  train travel 126
  travel agents 125
Trattoria La Grotta 115
travel agents 125
True Cross 86
tumulus 51
Tuscan Sun Festival 121

U

Ulysses 26
using the phone 126

V

Vasari 66
Vatican II Altar 149
veal cutlets 88
vicolo 29
visiting churches 135

W

wine tasting 138
workshop of 149
workshop of ... 60
Workshop of Signorelli 62, 63, 64

Cousin Nando slicing salsiccia and prosciutto for la cena.

Made in the USA
Las Vegas, NV
04 March 2022

45051297R00095